TAKING THE HIGH ROAD
to Reading, Writing, and Listening

Book 4

By Arlene Capriola and Rigmor Swensen

Phoenix Learning Resources

St. Louis • New York

ACKNOWLEDGEMENTS

Teachers at the Fifth Avenue Elementary School in East Northport, New York, expressed a need for supplementary materials to practice skills required for the new, more demanding curriculum. We responded to the request and spent many more hours than we had ever anticipated to create *Taking the High Road*.

The staff and students followed through, piloting and critiquing our manuscripts. To their credit, they made no concessions to our egos. They were very clear about what worked and what didn't.

Thank you, teachers and students at Fifth Avenue Elementary, and special thanks to Josephine Imwalle, Donna Marenus, and Francesca Montague. With gratitude and affection, we dedicate these books to all of you.

"The Snow Bird," from *Time for Poetry*, Scott Foresman, 1951
"The Bat," from *The Golden Treasury of Poetry*, Golden Press

Cover and interior page design: Pencil Point Studio
Illustrations: Ray Skibinski

Copyright © 1999 By Phoenix Learning Resources, Inc. All Rights Reserved. Printed in the United States of America. No part of this publication may be reproduced, stored in a retrieval system, or transmitted, in any form or by any means, electronic, mechanical, photocopying, recording, or otherwise, without prior written permission of the publisher.

ISBN: 0-7915-1649-0

3 4 5 6 7 8 9 0 03 02 01 00

TABLE OF CONTENTS

A Legend: **Betsy Ross and the American Flag** 1
    Objective Questions: Critical Thinking
    Using the Information: Short Answer Format
    Pre-Writing: Using a **5 W's Chart**
    Writing: Interview

A Poem: **The Snow Bird** 9
    Objective Questions: Critical Thinking
    Using the Information: Short Answer Format
    Pre-Writing: Using **Q.A.D. Notes**
    Writing: Descriptive Essay

A Biography: **Sacajawea Leads the Way** 17
    Objective Questions: Critical Thinking
    Using the Information: Short Answer Format
    Pre-Writing: Using a **Mind Map**
    Writing: Character Journal

A Correspondence: **A Letter to Billy** 25
    Objective Questions: Critical Thinking
    Using the Information: Short Answer Format
    Pre-Writing: Using a **Venn Diagram**
    Writing: Compare and Contrast

A Science Article: **Let's Go Spelunking** 33
    Objective Questions: Critical Thinking
    Using the Information: Short Answer Format
    Pre-Writing: Using a **Flow Chart**
    Writing: Sequence Story

A Social Studies Article **Marvelous Maps** 41
    Objective Questions: Critical Thinking
    Using the Information: Short Answer Format
    Pre-Writing: Using a **Reference Chart**
    Writing: Designing an Aerial Map

Listening Comprehension: **The Ridley Watch** 49
    Listening Directions: **Flow Chart**
    Using the Information: Short Answer Format
    Writing: Drawing a Conclusion

A Nordic Myth: **Why Do We Call It Thursday?** 53
    Objective Questions: Critical Thinking
    Using the Information: Short Answer Format
    Pre-Writing: Using a **Story Map**
    Writing: Problem and Solution

A Science Article: **Tornadoes—The Worst Storms on Earth** 61
    Objective Questions: Critical Thinking
    Using the Information: Short Answer Format
    Writing: Captions

Listening Comprehension: **An African Folktale, "How the World Got Wisdom"** 69
    Listening Directions: **Story Map**
    Using the Information: Short Answer Format
    Writing: Problem and Solution

A Social Studies Article: **The Boston Tea Party** 73
    Objective Questions: Critical Thinking
    Using the Information: Short Answer Format
    Pre-Writing: Using **Q.A.D. Notes**
    Writing: Descriptive Essay

A Study Skill: **Reading a Public Transportation Map** 81
    Objective Questions: Critical Thinking
    Pre-Writing: **Designing a Transportation Map**
    Writing: Asking Relevant Questions

A Poem: **The Bat** 85
    Objective Questions: Critical Thinking
    Using the Information: Short Answer Format
    Pre-Writing: Using a **Mind Map**
    Writing: Personal Narrative

A Biography: **Ben Franklin, Printer and More** 93
    Objective Questions: Critical Thinking
    Using the Information: Short Answer Format
    Pre-Writing: Using a **Mind Map**
    Writing: Newspaper Article

A Study Skill: **Reading a Time Line** 103
    Objective Questions: Critical Thinking
    Pre-Writing: **Designing a Time Line**
    Writing: Asking Relevant Questions

Editor's Page 107
Guide for **Revising** and **Editing** essays

A Legend

BETSY ROSS AND THE AMERICAN FLAG

What I Know

Fill in the correct circle.

1. The Revolutionary War was fought to _____.
   ○ win our freedom from England
   ○ force France to pay what they owed

2. The Congress of the United States _____.
   ○ elects the President
   ○ passes the laws that govern us

3. Someone who works in an upholstery shop _____.
   ○ washes and irons clothes
   ○ sews padded covering onto furniture

Check the Answer Box to see!

What I Want to Know

(✔ Check all that you want to know.)

❑ What Betsy Ross did
❑ Why Betsy's story is a legend
❑ Who designed the American flag
❑ What the first flag looked like
❑

(go on)

ANSWER BOX
1. The Revolutionary War was fought to win our freedom from England.
2. The Congress of the United States passes the laws that govern us.
3. A worker in an upholstery shop sews padded covering onto furniture.

BETSY ROSS AND THE AMERICAN FLAG

A legend is a story about a real person. Sometimes stories about that person are told and retold. As time goes by, some of the facts in the story change. Some of the storytellers add some new adventures to a person's life.

Betsy Ross was just such a person. She **resided**[1] in Philadelphia during the Revolutionary War. Betsy and her husband owned an upholstery shop. Most stories say that she designed and sewed the first American flag. But there is no real proof. Here is her story.

In the late 1700's the American colonists became more and more dissatisfied with British rule. They established, or formed, a new government. On April 19, 1775, the first battles of the Revolutionary War were fought. Betsy and John Ross opened their own shop that same year. The next year, John was **slain**[2] in the war.

Meanwhile, General George Washington had made up a small secret committee of three, consisting of himself, Robert Morris, and George Ross (Betsy's uncle). The purpose of this committee was to obtain a flag that would represent the United States of America. A new and different flag was necessary for several reasons. Ships at sea could identify themselves as American. The flag also would be a signal for the soldiers in battle. It would be a symbol of what the colonies were fighting for. It would **represent**[3] independence from England. When the war was over, it would show that the thirteen colonies were united as one nation.

Washington had already made an attempt to sketch the new flag.

[1]**resided**: lived
[2]**slain**: killed
[3]**represent**: stand for

He asked his two friends to help him get the flag made. Of course, George Ross thought of his niece, Betsy, right away. Off they went to her little shop.

Washington **envisioned**[4] a square flag with 13 red and white stripes and 13 stars. Each star was to have six points. But Betsy took one look at that sketch and said, "This square is not good. It will sway in the wind much more gracefully if it is a rectangle."

She studied it a little longer and said, "You will see that a five-pointed star is easier and prettier." She quickly folded some material and with one cut made a five-pointed star. The committee of three decided she knew exactly how to **proceed**[5], and off they went.

First Betsy went around town to see how other flags were made. She bought bunting, a special cloth used to make flags. Betsy sewed thirteen five-pointed stars in a circle on a blue field, or background. They stood for the thirteen colonies. She included thirteen red and white stripes.

The United States was born on July 4, 1776. Almost a year later, on June 14, 1777, a resolution, or decision, was passed in Congress. It said, "Resolved, that the flag of the United States be thirteen stripes alternate red and white, that the union be thirteen stars in a blue field, representing a new constellation."

We know that the first American flag had thirteen stars and stripes. We also know that Betsy Ross sewed for a living. But did she design and sew the first American flag? Was George Washington the one who asked her to make it? Is she the one who changed the stars from six points to five? All of this is part of the legend of Betsy Ross. But we'll never know for sure.

[4]**envisioned**: pictured or imagined
[5]**proceed**: go on

What I Learned

Circle the letter next to the answer you choose for each question.

1. Why is the story about Betsy Ross a legend?
   a. She did not live in Philadelphia.
   b. She sewed for a living.
   c. There is no proof.
   d. She never met George Washington.

2. Why was a flag necessary?
   a. Flags were used in parades.
   b. George Washington liked flags.
   c. The country was new.
   d. It helped people recognize a nation.

3. In this story, the word **field** refers to a _____ .
   a. place to play sports
   b. place where crops are grown
   c. background
   d. kind of legend

4. What did Betsy correct on George Washington's sketch?
   a. the shape
   b. the colors
   c. the size
   d. the stripes

5. What did the stars on the flag represent?
   a. the nighttime sky
   b. the 13 colonies
   c. the years of the war
   d. the brightness of day

6. Congress passed a resolution to adopt the flag. This means that _____ .
   a. Congress changed the colors
   b. it decided to accept the flag
   c. people talked about the flag
   d. the flag was refused

7. What is the setting for this story?
   a. the Civil War
   b. England long ago
   c. South America
   d. the American Revolution

8. Which of these happened AFTER the "birth" of our country?
   a. John and Betsy opened a shop.
   b. The Revolutionary War began.
   c. Congress agreed on the flag.
   d. John Ross was killed.

Using the Information
Write a short paragraph for each question below.

Be sure to use details from the story in your answer!

1. Do you think Betsy Ross really made the first flag? Explain.

_____

_____

_____

_____

2. According to the story, what steps did Betsy take to make the flag?

_____

_____

_____

_____

Using the Information

3. Describe the first American flag.

_____

_____

_____

_____

4. What does the U.S. flag look like now? Draw it.

Pre-Writing Pretend you are a colonial newspaper reporter sent to interview Betsy Ross. She has already said that she did sew the first American flag. What else about the legend do you want to know? Fill in the 5 W's Chart below with questions that will give you the answers.

You may NOT ask yes/no questions!

1. **Who** asked you to design the first American flag?

2. **When** did _____

3. **Where** did _____

4. **Why** did you _____

5. **What** colors _____

6. **How** did you _____

7. _____

Add another question!

7

Writing Now change roles. You are Betsy Ross. Write at least one full sentence in answer to each of the questions the reporter has asked.

Use your imagination! Let some answers be different from the legend!

Go to Editor's Page

A Poem
THE SNOW-BIRD

What I Know

Fill in the correct circle.

1. The small birds, seen often in winter, are called _____ .
   - ○ robins
   - ○ snow-birds

2. If the rhyming lines on a poem are 1 & 3 and 2 & 4, we say that it has an _____ .
   - ○ a c, b d rhyming pattern
   - ○ a b, c d rhyming pattern

3. This poem has three stanzas. This means it has _____ .
   - ○ three parts
   - ○ three rhyming lines

Check the Answer Box to see!

What I Want to Know

(✔ Check all that you want to know.)

- ❏ What the snow-bird is doing
- ❏ How the poet feels about the bird
- ❏ What the bird eats in winter

(go on)

ANSWER BOX
1. The small birds, seen often in winter, are called snow-birds.
2. If the rhyming lines on a poem are 1 & 3 and 2 & 4, we say that it has an a c, b d rhyming pattern.
3. If a poem has three stanzas, it has three parts.

9

THE SNOW-BIRD

This poem tells about a bird in winter. Look for the rhyming pattern. Read the poem carefully at least two times before answering the questions.

When all the ground with snow is white,
The merry snow-bird comes,
And hops about with great delight
To find the scattered crumbs.

How glad he seems to get to eat
A piece of cake or bread!
He wears no shoes upon his feet,
Nor hat upon his head.

But happiest is he, I know,
Because no cage with bars
Keeps him from walking on the snow
And printing it with stars.

by Frank Dempster Sherman

What I Learned

Circle the letter next to the answer you choose for each question.

1. This poem takes place in the _____.
   a. winter
   b. spring
   c. summer
   d. night

2. What makes the bird the happiest?
   a. It is snowing.
   b. He is free.
   c. He sees the food.
   d. He has no hat or shoes.

3. When the poet says that the bird is "printing [the snow] with stars," it means _____.
   a. he is dropping stars
   b. the bread is star-shaped
   c. the snow has stars in it
   d. his feet form a star pattern

4. We can tell that the setting for this poem is _____.
   a. the southern U.S.
   b. somewhere up North
   c. on a desert island
   d. at the Equator

5. We know that the bird is not alone because _____.
   a. there is a cage nearby
   b. other birds are with him
   c. there is a cat watching him
   d. someone is telling what he does

6. What did the poet probably do just before this poem?
   a. went to bed
   b. played in the snow
   c. sprinkled crumbs outside
   d. made stars in the snow

7. What is the mood of this poem?
   a. quiet and peaceful
   b. funny
   c. sad and sorrowful
   d. exciting

8. How can we tell that the poet likes birds?
   a. He cages them.
   b. He has a house for them.
   c. He gives them stars.
   d. He feeds them.

Using the Information Write a short paragraph for each question below.

Be sure to use details from the poem in your answer!

1. Why are bread crumbs so important to a bird in winter?

_____

_____

_____

_____

2. Explain why the snow-bird is happy.

_____

_____

_____

_____

Using the Information

3. How do you think the poet feels about nature?

_____

_____

_____

_____

4. Draw a picture of how the snow looks **before** the snow-bird comes.

Pre-Writing

By studying this poem we can tell a lot about the poet.
We know that he is a man and that he enjoys feeding and watching birds. What else is he like?
Use your imagination to create a character sketch that tells about the poet.
Use the Q.A.D. form below.

Remember to add lots of interesting details!

Question	Answer	Details
1. How old is he?		
2. What does he look like?		
3. What type of job does he have?		
4. Who does he live with?		

Question	Answer	Details
5. What is his house like?		
6. Where is he when he is writing this?		
7. What one word best describes him?		

Make an Illustration

Use your Q.A.D. notes to show Mr. Sherman and his family in their home.

Writing Use your Q.A.D. notes and illustration to write a paragraph about this poet. Your first sentence is the topic sentence and should tell about him in a general way. (Use your answer to Question # 7 to help you.)

..."like "Mr. Sherman is very observant."

Go to Editor's Page

A Biography

SACAJAWEA LEADS THE WAY

What I Know

Fill in the correct circle.

1. An interpreter is someone who _____ .
   - ○ moves from place to place
   - ○ translates words to another language

2. Lewis and Clark were famous _____ .
   - ○ teachers
   - ○ explorers

3. Before Lewis and Clark's expedition, Americans _____ the Northwest Territory.
   - ○ knew very little about
   - ○ wanted to buy

Check the Answer Box to see!

What I Want to Know

(✔ Check all that you want to know.)

- ❑ Who Sacajawea was
- ❑ Why Sacajawea is famous
- ❑ What Lewis and Clark explored
- ❑ What surprise Sacajawea found
- ❑ _____→

(go on)

ANSWER BOX
1. An interpreter is someone who translates words to another language.
2. Lewis and Clark were famous explorers.
3. Before Lewis and Clark's expedition, Americans knew very little about the Northwest Territory.

SACAJAWEA LEADS THE WAY

Just at the time Sacajawea, a Shoshone Indian girl, was growing up, Americans were getting curious about America. The States were independent. Now they wanted to know what land lay to the west of the colonies.

In 1803, President Thomas Jefferson asked Lewis and Clark to explore the uncharted land from the Mississippi River to the Pacific Ocean. Their journey was called the Lewis and Clark Expedition. Their success was mostly due to their brave guide, Sacajawea. Because of the many strange events that happened in her life, Sacajawea was the perfect person to lead them through this unmapped territory.

Sacajawea's tribe, the Shoshones, were nomads, people who moved from place to place and lived in tepees. They followed trails through the mountains and plains to hunt buffalo. So Sacajawea knew where to find wild plants and fruits to eat.

One day, the Shoshones were attacked by an enemy tribe and fourteen-year-old Sacajawea was captured. She became a slave for the Mandan Indian tribe that lived in what is now North Dakota. They taught her how to cook and make medicine from plants. She learned their language well.

When she was sixteen, the Mandans sold her to Mr. Charbonneau. He was a French fur trader and interpreter who loved Sacajawea. In May, 1804, the Lewis and Clark expedition set out from St. Louis, up the Missouri River. Mr. Charbonneau was asked to be their interpreter as they explored the Northwest. Sacajawea tied her baby to her back and the little family set out with the group.

Sacajawea cooked and washed clothes. She took care of the men when they were sick. She spoke Shoshone, Mandan, French, and English. She could tell Captain Clark about trails and villages she knew about from her childhood.

Then her wildest dreams came true. Sacajawea and the men came to a village where her brother was the chief. What a joyful reunion it was! Because of her, the Shoshones listened carefully to Lewis and Clark's plan. They gave them horses to cross the high Rocky Mountains. In addition, they sent along extra guides to help the explorers get through the mountains to the Columbia River.

The expedition started out again in August, 1805. Although it was not yet autumn, the Rocky Mountains' freezing snow and biting sleet and rain blocked the trails. The skillful Indian guides found other ways. Safely on the western side of this mountain range, Sacajawea once again took over, and one day in November, they reached the shores of the Pacific Ocean. The American flag was raised to the top of the tallest tree.

Because of Sacajawea's help, the Northwest Territory was claimed for the United States. Our country now truly reached from ocean to ocean, across the whole continent. Captain Clark thanked her. He said they would never have found their way without her. Sacajawea was the first American woman to cross the Rocky Mountains and the first one to see the Pacific Ocean.

What I Learned

Circle the letter next to the answer you choose for each question.

1. This story is mainly about _____ .
   a. exploring
   b. an Indian guide
   c. hunting buffalo
   d. the American flag

2. Why were the Shoshones called nomads?
   a. They went where the buffalo went.
   b. They built small cities.
   c. They stayed in one place.
   d. They had big families.

3. Before Sacajawea was captured by the Mandans, she _____ .
   a. was sold to Mr. Charbonneau
   b. was a Shoshone
   c. was an Indian guide
   d. learned their language

4. What would probably NOT have happened today?
   a. People would go exploring.
   b. There would be snow in the Rockies.
   c. Interpreters would be needed.
   d. Sacajawea would be sold to a trader.

5. How did Lewis and Clark get across the Rockies?
   a. They had special guides.
   b. The river helped them.
   c. They had a map made at the fort.
   d. They had good weather.

6. Why was Sacajawea such a good guide?
   a. She liked to travel.
   b. She spoke many languages.
   c. She liked Lewis and Clark.
   d. She went to school.

7. What kind of person was Sacajawea?
   a. angry
   b. very silly
   c. sad
   d. very smart

8. What did the United States claim because of Sacajawea's help?
   a. jewels and oil
   b. a large piece of land
   c. an American flag
   d. the Pacific Ocean

Using the Information

Write a short paragraph for each question below.

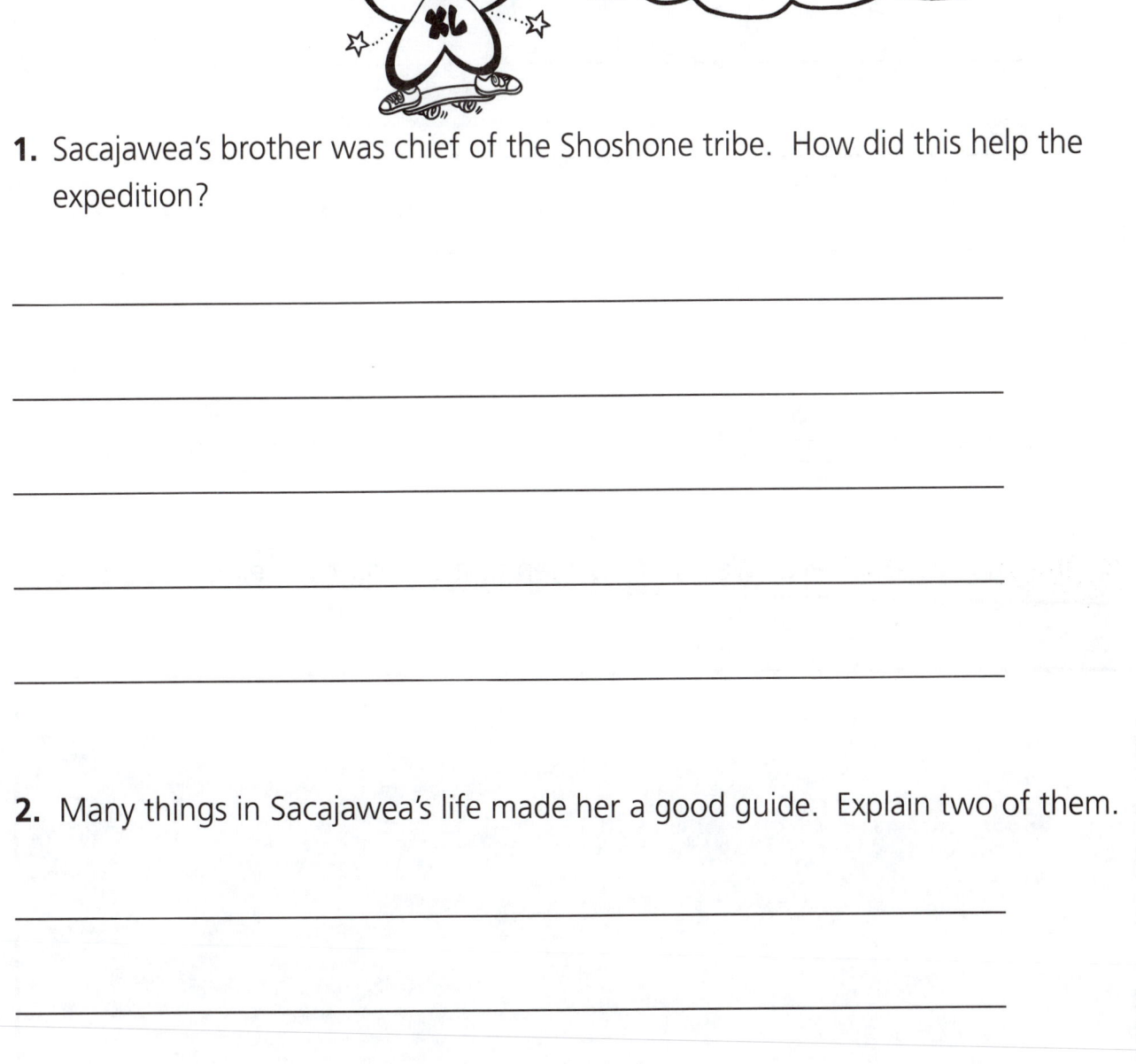

Be sure to use details from the story

1. Sacajawea's brother was chief of the Shoshone tribe. How did this help the expedition?

_____
_____
_____
_____

2. Many things in Sacajawea's life made her a good guide. Explain two of them.

_____
_____
_____

Using the Information

3. Why was the Northwest Territory so important to the U.S.?

_____

_____

_____

_____

_____

4. Draw a picture of Sacajawea and the men at the end of the expedition.

Pre-Writing You are there! You are with the Lewis and Clark expedition when Sacajawea meets her brother after many, many years. What is their meeting like?
Fill in the Mind Map below with notes you have jotted down. Write it in the third person, (using "he", "she", "they"), as though you are watching what is happening.

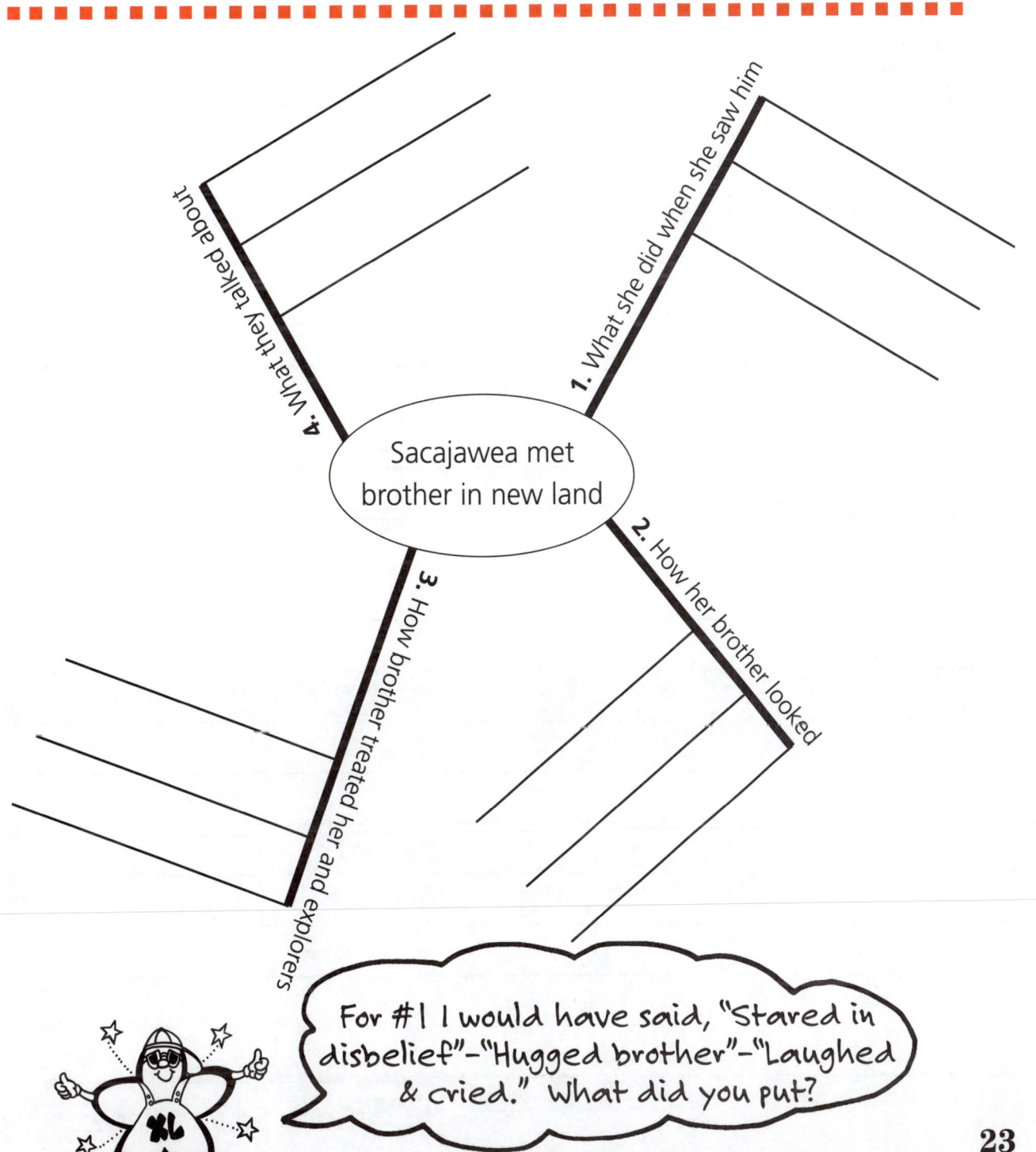

Center: Sacajawea met brother in new land
1. What she did when she saw him
2. How her brother looked
3. How brother treated her and explorers
4. What they talked about

For #1 I would have said, "Stared in disbelief"–"Hugged brother"–"Laughed & cried." What did you put?

23

Writing Use your notes about Sacajawea's meeting with her brother to write your journal. Remember, people will be reading about this important event hundreds of years from now when our country has 50 states!

You'll be famous!

Go to Editor's Page

Correspondence
A LETTER TO BILLY

What I Know

Fill in the correct circle.

1. Illinois is the name of a _____ in the United States.
   ○ city   ○ state

2. If you are on a traveling soccer team, you may have to _____ .
   ○ sleep far from home   ○ move every two years

3. If you live in an **urban** area, you live _____ .
   ○ in a city   ○ in the country

What I Want to Know

(✔ Check all that you want to know.)

- ❏ Who wrote to Billy
- ❏ What the letter said
- ❏ Who's on a traveling team
- ❏ Where the traveling team went
- ❏ _____→

(go on)

ANSWER BOX
1. Illinois is the name of a state in the United States.
2. If you are on a traveling soccer team, you may have to sleep far from home.
3. If you live in an urban area, you live in a city.

A LETTER TO BILLY

August 1, _____

Dear Billy,

I am having a wonderful time on my train trip across the United States. Everyone on my traveling soccer team comes from a different part of Illinois. It is such fun to talk with them. Billy, you would really like my two new soccer friends, Joe and Miguel.

Joe comes from a small town. Although the town is small, there are one thousand kids in his school. It has three separate low buildings. The kids travel in from farms outside town and from small villages nearby. They make up games to entertain themselves on the long bus ride to school every day.

Joe loves to play soccer, so he stays after school for practice. It is almost always dark when the late bus takes him home. There is a big soccer field in the back of the school. On Saturday mornings, when they have a game, almost the whole town comes out to watch.

Miguel lives in an urban area, Chicago. He goes to a large school, too. It is three stories high. However, all the kids live right in the neighborhood. They walk to school every day.

Miguel darts home for a snack before soccer practice in the afternoon. His team plays league games on Saturday. Across the street from his school, there is a park where they put up goals each time there is a game. Most of the time, only the family of the players come out to see the games.

So far our team has won three games and tied for one. We haven't lost a game yet! This is the best summer ever! I think I've found two great new friends! You'd really like them, too. I've told them that you and I make great teammates on the field. You should think about signing up for this team next year.

See you in about three weeks.

Your pal,

Larry

What I Learned

Circle the letter next to the answer you choose for each question.

1. How are Joe and Miguel alike?
   - a. They live in small towns.
   - b. They live in big cities.
   - c. They like to play soccer.
   - d. They are on the bus.

2. How can you tell that Miguel lives near his school?
   - a. He rides the bus.
   - b. He runs home for a snack.
   - c. He likes soccer.
   - d. He is always late.

3. Why does Joe's school have as many kids as Miguel's school?
   - a. There are many people in town.
   - b. The school is very big.
   - c. They can walk to school.
   - d. They come from many towns.

4. When do Joe and Miguel practice?
   - a. They both practice after school.
   - b. They both practice in the gym.
   - c. They both practice in the park.
   - d. They both practice in the morning.

5. What do Joe and Miguel share about where they live?
   - a. They live in town.
   - b. They live in a city.
   - c. They live in the same state.
   - d. They live on a farm.

6. What is different about Joe's soccer games?
   - a. Almost everyone comes.
   - b. Only the families come.
   - c. Mostly kids come.
   - d. Mostly grown-ups come.

7. How much longer will Larry's trip take?
   - a. about thirty weeks
   - b. about three days
   - c. until next summer
   - d. about three weeks

8. What do you think Billy will probably do next year?
   - a. join the Boy Scouts
   - b. go to school in Chicago
   - c. stop playing soccer
   - d. join the traveling team

Using the Information Write a short paragraph for each question below.

Be sure to use details from the letter in your answer!

1. Why do you think Billy will find this letter interesting?

_____

_____

_____

_____

2. What part does the game of soccer play in this story?

_____

_____

_____

_____

Using the Information

3. What is *your* community like?

_____

_____

_____

_____

4. Draw a picture of the travel team on the way to the next game.

Pre-Writing

Larry's two new friends both love soccer, but they are different in many ways. We can show how things are alike and different with a **Venn diagram**. Compare the two boys in the Venn Diagram below. Show <u>at least</u> five ways the two boys are alike and five ways they are different.

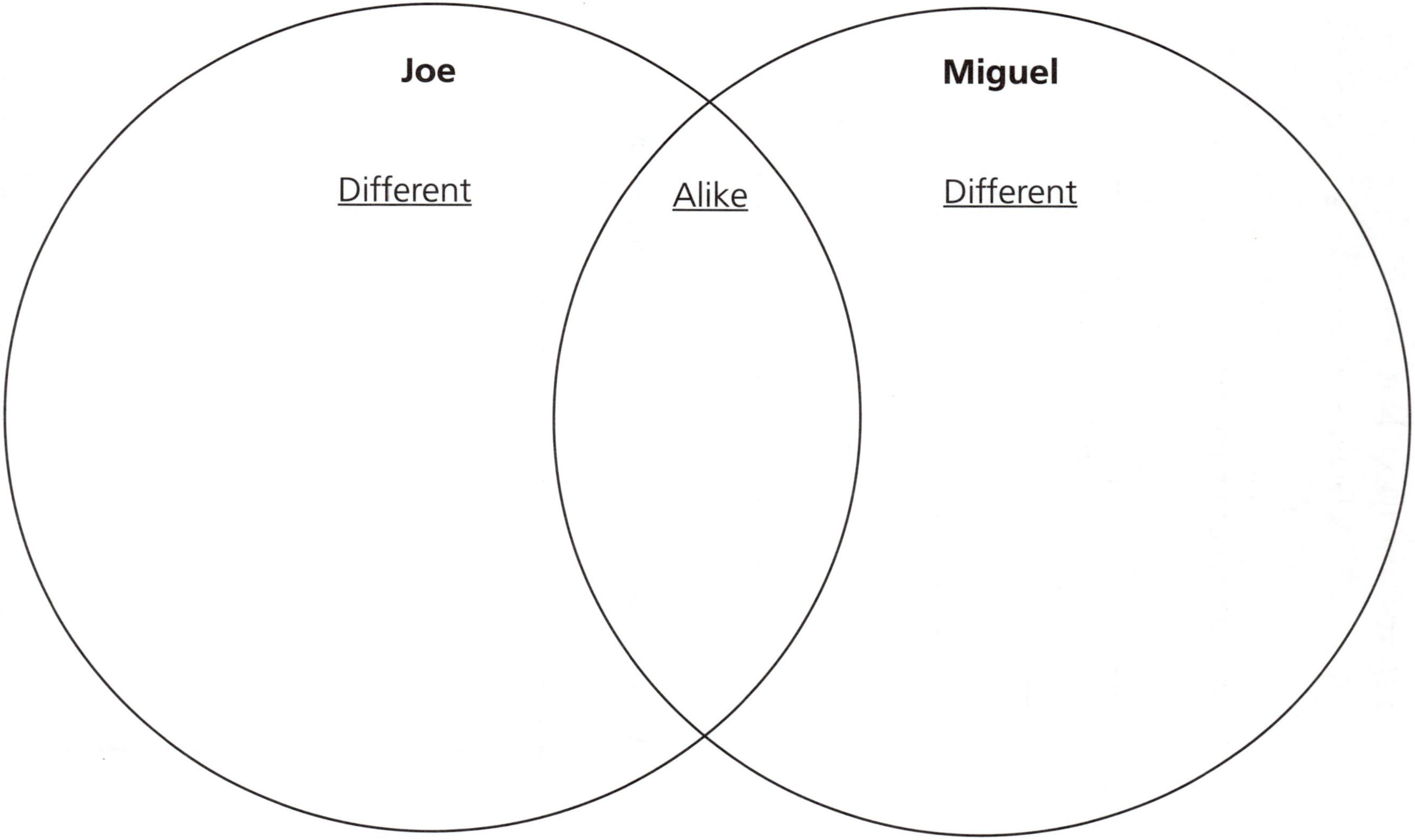

Miguel

<u>Different</u>

<u>Alike</u>

Joe

<u>Different</u>

Writing Write one paragraph showing how the two boys' lives are alike and one paragraph showing ways that they are different. Begin each paragraph with a good topic sentence. Then follow with the information from your Venn Diagram.

Do you think they are more alike? or more different?

Go to Editor's Page

An Illustration Pictures make good comparisons. In the boxes below, show at least one way that Joe's and Miguel's school experiences are different and one way they are the same. Label the things you show in your pictures.

Alike

Different

A Science Article
LET'S GO SPELUNKING

What I Know

Fill in the correct circle.

1. When you go spelunking, you are _____ .
   ○ in a museum   ○ inside a cave

2. A nocturnal animal is _____ .
   ○ active at night   ○ a tame house pet

3. This article states that part of the cave is "completely dark." Can animals live here?
   ○ yes   ○ no

Check the Answer Box to see!

What I Want to Know

(✔ Check all that you want to know.)

❑ Which animals live in caves
❑ What the inside smells like
❑ What grows inside caves
❑ Where you can go spelunking
❑ _____

(go on)

ANSWER BOX
1. When you go spelunking, you are inside a cave.
2. A nocturnal animal is active at night.
3. Yes, some animals can live in complete darkness.

33

LET'S GO SPELUNKING

Dressed for spelunking

Would you like to go spelunking? Let's take an imaginary trip with a spelunker, exploring deep into caves. You need a miner's helmet lamp that throws a big circle of light, that will cover the floors, the walls, and the ceiling. Take along a flashlight with some extra batteries as a backup. Just to be safe, bring some candles and matches in case the helmet lamp goes out.

THE TWILIGHT ZONE

First you walk into the twilight zone. It's a little cooler than outside and it is the only part of the cave which still receives some daylight. You'll spot wildflowers, and plants, like ferns and moss, in the twilight zone. Here is the red cave salamander and the brown slimy salamander which lays its eggs in damp caves. At night, wood rats, barn owls, and snakes slip out for nocturnal hunting.

Animals on a nocturnal hunt

34

THE MIDDLE REGION

Next you enter an area that is even darker. Here the temperature doesn't change much. It is chilly and damp and there is a **dank**[1], stale smell in the air. Mushrooms grow here. Bats sleep here during the day. They hang down from the roof. At night, they fly out to hunt for food. Their eyes can see, but not in the darkness of the cave. So each one has its own special high squeak that echoes back to its ears. In a way, its ears act like eyes.

DEEP INSIDE

Then, you reach the deepest part of the cave. It is completely dark and **still**[2]. The temperature never changes. The salamanders that live here have no color and cannot see. You will find that the crickets are blind and pale, but they have long **antennae**[3] on their heads, which sense food. The female crickets bury their eggs. But the blind beetles can smell them and dig to locate and eat them. Animals in the deepest part of the cave use touch, sound, and taste to find food.

Flashlights reveal the Deep Inside

Finally, it is time to find your way out again. The bright light of day may hurt your eyes at first, but you will soon readjust. If you ever want to go spelunking, certain parks have caves. You can go on a tour with a leader who will explain all about caves.

[1]**dank**: damp
[2]**still**: quiet
[3]**antennae**: feelers on the head

What I Learned

Circle the letter next to the answer you choose for each question.

1. What is this article mainly about?
   - a. discovering bats
   - b. exploring caves
   - c. walking in darkness
   - d. taking vacations

2. What does the twilight zone look like?
   - a. It is sunny.
   - b. It is completely dark.
   - c. It is cloudy.
   - d. There is very dim light.

3. Animals that hunt at night are _____.
   - a. afraid
   - b. slimy
   - c. nocturnal
   - d. blind

4. What might you see BEFORE you reach the deepest part of the cave?
   - a. bats upside down
   - b. crickets with long antennae
   - c. blind beetles
   - d. salamanders with no color

5. Which one of the senses does the bat use most?
   - a. hearing
   - b. seeing
   - c. touching
   - d. smelling

6. Why are the animals in the deepest part of the cave blind?
   - a. They have been hurt.
   - b. They do not need to see.
   - c. They sleep a lot.
   - d. They do not hunt.

7. How are the animals in the twilight zone different from those in the deepest zone?
   - a. They leave the cave sometimes.
   - b. They have no color.
   - c. They cannot see.
   - d. They do not eat.

8. This article shows that creatures make use of the _____ they need most.
   - a. air
   - b. water
   - c. time
   - d. senses

Using the Information
Write a short paragraph for each question below:

Be sure to use details from the story in your answer!

1. What preparations do you have to make to be a spelunker?

_____

_____

_____

_____

2. How do you think the first part of a cave got the name, "The Twilight Zone"?

_____

_____

_____

_____

Using the Information

3. Tell one fact you remember about each part of the cave.

_____

_____

_____

_____

_____

4. Draw a picture of an animal that lives in the middle region of a cave.

Pre-Writing This article takes you step-by-step through a cave. It uses the words **first, next, then,** and **finally** to show you the sequence of events. Think of a trip that you have taken—with your family, class, club, or alone. Then fill in the Flow Chart below showing the events as they happened.

Write short notes only. Do not write in sentences!

First _____
(Tell what you did.)
_____
(Tell what you saw, heard, felt, smelled, tasted, etc.)

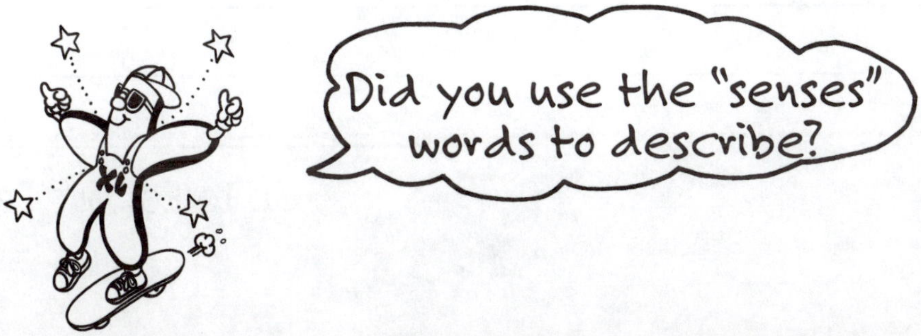

Did you use the "senses" words to describe?

39

Writing You are ready to write your story of your trip. Use your notes to help you keep the events in order. Put them into full sentences.
- Use the sequence words in the story or choose your own.
- Remember to tell what you saw, heard, felt, smelled, tasted, etc.

Some other good sequence words are: later, later on, after that, afterwards, at last!

Go to Editor's Page

A Social Studies Article
MARVELOUS MAPS

What I Know

Fill in the correct circle.

1. A building or tree that helps you locate a place is called a ____ .
   ○ landmark   ○ historical site

2. Words in the text such as **is**, **are**, **called**, **or**, **means**, and **which** are special signal words. They tell you that a _____ is in the sentence.
   ○ definition   ○ proper noun

3. Maps need to change when the _____ .
   ○ time changes   ○ Earth changes

Check the Answer Box to see!

What I Want to Know

(✔ Check all that you want to know.)

❑ What the different types of maps are
❑ How we can tell what the symbols on a map mean
❑ How maps can change
❑ _____→

(go on)

ANSWER BOX
1. A building or tree that helps you locate a place is called a landmark.
2. Words such as **is**, **are**, **called or**, **means**, and **which** tell you that a definition is in the sentence.
3. Maps need to change when the Earth changes.

41

MARVELOUS MAPS

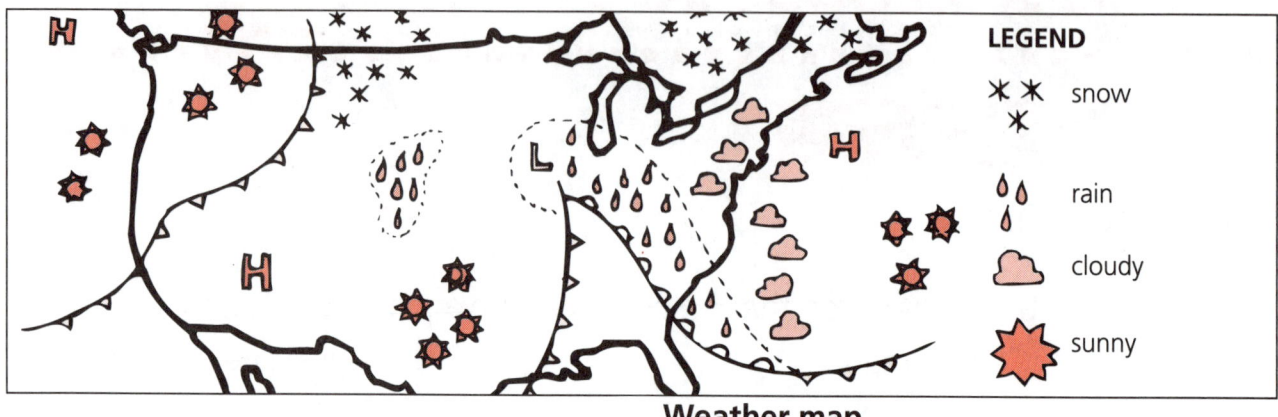

Weather map

There probably never was a time when maps didn't exist. People have always needed to get directions to another place. Probably the very first maps were just drawn into the dirt or sand or snow with a stick. They probably showed special buildings, trees, rivers, or other **landmarks** to help people along the way.

People have always been curious. New kinds of maps were designed as people came to know more and more about the world. Maps of the oceans, called **maritime** maps, were drawn for sailors. Sky maps show the heavens, and satellites have even given us the ability to make maps of the moon. A new friend might sketch you a map to find your way to his or her house.

Maps can be fascinating because they can tell us so many things about a place. A map needs a **legend**. The legend is usually in a box at the side or bottom of a map and is an explanation of the **symbols** used on a map. A map would get very crowded if words had to be written for every railroad line, mountain range, airport, or camping grounds. So symbols are made to stand for those things. A double line might show a main highway. A tiny plane would show the location of an airport. Lots of little green triangles would tell you there is a forest. A capital letter **P** means there is a parking space at that location.

The legend also tells the **scale** of the map. For example, there might be a short line on the legend and it would say 1 inch=100 miles. Map makers need to do this so that the map of a whole country can fit on one page. The legend also explains what colors are used for. Sometimes, on a **political** map, each state or country is in a different color. Water is usually blue.

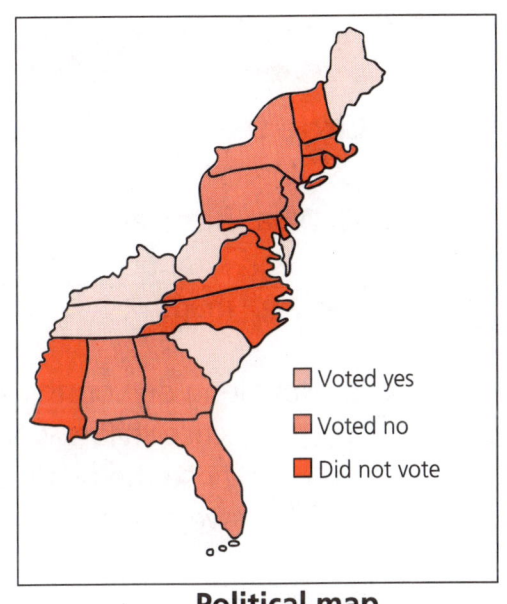
Political map

The symbols in a legend depend on what kind of map you are looking at. Road maps tell you about streets and directions. Other maps point out camping places or historical spots. There are maps that show where crops are grown. Weather maps are in the newspaper and on TV every day.

Today **aerial** maps, which are photographs taken from airplanes or satellites, are sent to a computer. These computers draw **topographical** maps which show the exact shape of the land. Mountains, valleys, rivers, highways, bridges, and dams appear on these maps. The earth changes because of floods, earthquakes, mud slides, and other acts of nature.

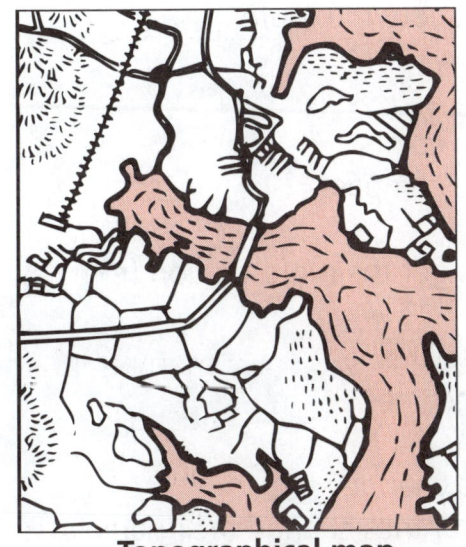
Topographical map

As you can see, maps change all the time. Political maps have to be changed because countries get new borders and new names. Weather maps change every day. Topographical maps change because nature changes the Earth and because people build new roads, bridges, and dams.

What I Learned

Circle the letter next to the answer you choose for each question.

1. What is this article mainly about?
   a. symbols
   b. legends
   c. maps
   d. landmarks

2. How long do you think maps have existed?
   a. since sailors went to sea
   b. since writing was invented
   c. since the first roads were built
   d. since the earliest people

3. Why does a map need a legend?
   a. to tell the story
   b. to explain the symbols used
   c. to name the map
   d. to explain photographs

4. Why does a map use symbols?
   a. to make it colorful
   b. to save space
   c. to show the politics
   d. to show the route

5. What explains the distances on a map?
   a. the scale of miles
   b. the colors
   c. the tiny airplanes
   d. the compass

6. Computers that draw topographical maps get their information from _____ .
   a. landmarks
   b. satellites
   c. mountains
   d. time lines

7. Which of these is NOT a reason that maps change?
   a. Weather changes every day.
   b. Countries change their names.
   c. Earthquakes change the earth.
   d. New Presidents are elected.

8. If you were going out on a boat, which map would you need?
   a. a sky map
   b. an aerial map
   c. a maritime map
   d. a political map

44

Using the Information Write a short paragraph for each question below.

Be sure to use details from the story in your answer!

1. Tell about three kinds of maps. Explain their uses.

_____
_____
_____
_____

2. Why do cartographers have to continue making new maps?

_____
_____
_____
_____

45

Using the Information This article told about four different types of maps. A Reference Chart is useful when you need to remember and use many different types of things. Fill in the missing parts of the chart below.

Type of Map	What It Shows	One Thing It Could Show Is…	A Good Symbol for It Is…
Maritime	heavens satellites	Big Dipper	
Political			
Aerial		forests	
Topographical			

46

Pre-Writing Draw an aerial map of a park.
- In the legend, draw the symbols you use.
- Fill in the scale below.

Legend

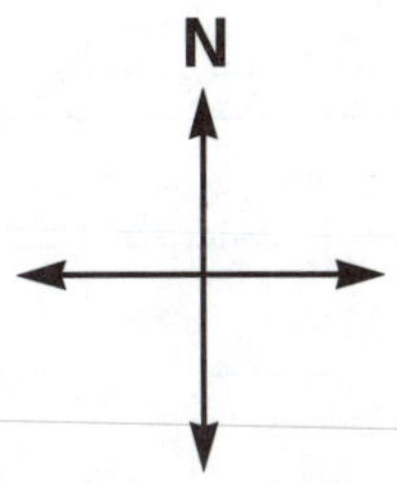

N

1 inch = ___ feet

47

Writing Use the information in your aerial map to describe your park.

Go to Editor's Page

Listening Comprehension
THE RIDLEY WATCH

Listening Directions
Listen to the story "The Ridley Watch." The first time you hear it, listen carefully but do not take notes. The second time you hear the story, write brief notes in the **flow chart**, below. These notes will help you answer some questions about the story.

49

Using the Information Write a short paragraph for each question below.

Be sure to use details from the story in your answer!

1. Explain what Jane meant when she said, "This little turtle is cold stunned. Otherwise it would have found its way to the ocean already."

_____

_____

_____

_____

2. What point did Jane want to make when she talked about shivering after swimming? How did this help them with the turtle?

_____

_____

_____

_____

Using the Information

3. Explain what you think happened to the ridley after the ranger picked it up.

_____

_____

_____

_____

4. Draw a picture of Jane and Paul returning the turtle to the ocean.

Writing Which lesson below does this story teach best?
- ○ It is good to be an environmentalist.
- ○ Sometimes it is better to get expert help than to do something by yourself.

Write an essay explaining why you chose this lesson. Use the story details in your flow chart to help you.

Go to Editor's Page

A Nordic Myth

WHY DO WE CALL IT THURSDAY?

What I Know

Fill in the correct circle.

1. The Vikings were people who lived about _____ .
   ○ 200 years ago   ○ 1000 years ago

2. The Vikings believed in _____ .
   ○ one god   ○ many gods

3. If a story discusses giants and magic hammers, we can tell that it is _____ .
   ○ nonfiction   ○ fiction

Check the Answer Box to see!

What I Want to Know

(✔ Check all that you want to know.)

❑ How Thursday got its name
❑ What Nordic myths are
❑ Who the Viking gods were
❑ Why people made up myths
❑ _____
(go on) →

ANSWER BOX
1. The Vikings were people who lived about 1000 years ago.
2. The Vikings believed in many gods.
3. A story that discusses giants and magic hammers is fiction.

53

WHY DO WE CALL IT THURSDAY?

The Norse myths were told by the Vikings, who lived in the north of Europe a thousand years ago. What caused floods and famine? Why were some people healthy and others ill? What could people do to try to control nature? Myths and magic were the science of those days. They were stories that tried to explain how the world began and what people and nature were all about. The Vikings believed their gods and goddesses had supernatural powers.

THOR, THE GOD OF THUNDER

This is a story about the god Thor. He was such a famous god that the day of the week, Thursday, was named after him. He had a long red beard and wild blue eyes. Thor traveled across the sky in a chariot pulled by two enormous goats. He was the strongest of the gods, so they chose him to defend Asgard, the home of the gods.

Of course, he didn't do this without help. Three magic things made him mighty. Thor's magic hammer, Miolnir, always smashed the intended target. People believed that's what caused the roar of thunder in the skies. Miolnir was like a boomerang; it always flew back to Thor's strong magic gloves. Thor also possessed a magic belt. When he put it on he grew twice as strong as he already was.

THRYM THE GIANT

One morning Thor woke up to find that his hammer had been stolen by the giant, Thrym. Thrym said he would only give it back if Freya, the beautiful goddess, would marry him.

Now, goddesses had never married giants. And Thrym was an especially ugly giant. But everyone agreed that Thor had to have his hammer back. The gods held a meeting to plan a strategy. They told Thrym it was a deal; he could have Freya if she received Miolnir as a wedding gift.

Thrym got so excited that he arranged a splendid wedding celebration. Freya, dressed with a veil over her face, arrived at the feast. Thrym requested a greeting kiss. But Freya whispered she was too shy to be kissed before she married.

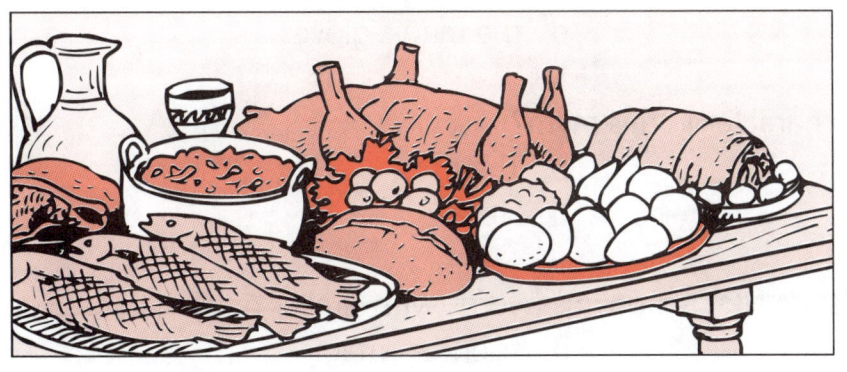

At dinner, Freya ate a huge ox, several salmon, a table full of vegetables, and almost all the desserts. Thrym couldn't believe his eyes and stared at her in amazement. Freya whispered that she had been so excited about her approaching wedding day, that she had not had a morsel of food to eat for a week.

After the feast, Thrym thought that it was time for a kiss from his bride. But Freya stated she wanted Thrym to keep his word. Miolnir, the hammer, was to be her bride's gift, and she wanted it before the wedding.

Thrym rushed off to get Miolnir for his bride. No sooner had he placed it across her knees, than she jumped up and ripped off the veil. There was Thor! He had come, dressed up like Freya. With Miolnir in his possession, Thor fought his way out of Thrym's castle, killing all the giants as he went.

So Thursday is Thor's day. Thor was the god of thunder who managed to get his magic hammer back by pretending to be a bride.

What I Learned

Circle the letter next to the answer you choose for each question.

1. Where did this story take place?
   - a. in the South
   - b. by the sea
   - c. in an imaginary world
   - d. on another planet

2. Why did the Vikings tell myths?
   - a. to explain things they didn't understand
   - b. to write history
   - c. to sell things
   - d. to please the gods

3. The Vikings used Miolnir to explain _____.
   - a. Freya's big appetite
   - b. how gods travel
   - c. thunder
   - d. the magic gloves

4. Who is the main character in this myth?
   - a. Miolnir
   - b. Thrym
   - c. Thor
   - d. Freya

5. Which two words are NOT synonyms (words with similar meanings)?
   - a. myths—stories
   - b. science—magic
   - c. enormous—big
   - d. magic—supernatural

6. What was the main problem or conflict?
   - a. Thrym was a giant.
   - b. Freya didn't love Thrym.
   - c. Thor needed to get his hammer back.
   - d. The thunder was too loud.

7. How did Thor try to solve the problem?
   - a. by buying back Miolnir
   - b. by kissing Thrym
   - c. by playing a trick
   - d. by eating a lot

8. What do we have today that reminds us of the god Thor?
   - a. hammers
   - b. giants
   - c. magic
   - d. Thursday

Using the Information Write a short paragraph for each question below.

Be sure to use details from the story in your answer!

1. Describe Thor's three magic helpers.

_____

_____

_____

_____

_____

2. Why do you think Thrym stole the hammer from Thor?

_____

_____

_____

_____

Using the Information

3. Explain how Thor tricked Thrym.

_____

_____

_____

_____

_____

4. Draw a picture of Thor on the wedding day.

58

Pre-Writing A Story Map allows us to organize the important facts of the story. Fill in the story map below for the myth of Thor.

Use note form. Don't write in full sentences!

Title: _____

Setting: _____

Characters: _____

Problem: _____

_____

Events: _____

_____

_____

_____

Solution: _____

_____

Writing Use your story map to describe Thor's problem.
Then explain how he solves it, using details from the story.
Change your notes to full sentences and add descriptive words.

Keep your summary short. Don't go past this page!

Go to Editor's Page

A Science Article

TORNADOES: THE WORST STORMS ON EARTH

What I Know

Fill in the correct circle.

1. A tornado is a _____ .
   - ○ wild whirling wind
   - ○ fierce rain storm

2. This article says, "The funnel-shaped cloud, or vortex, of the thundercloud does not touch the ground." We can tell from the sentence that a vortex is a _____ .
   - ○ thundercloud
   - ○ funnel-shaped cloud

3. When you forecast something, you _____ .
   - ○ make a mold
   - ○ predict

Check the Answer Box to see!

What I Want to Know

(✔ Check all that you want to know.)

- ❑ How tornadoes form
- ❑ Where they usually take place
- ❑ How long they last
- ❑ Why they are still a mystery
- ❑ _____

(go on)

ANSWER BOX
1. A tornado is a wild whirling wind.
2. We can tell from this sentence that a vortex is a funnel-shaped cloud.
3. When you forecast something, you predict.

61

TORNADOES: THE WORST STORMS ON EARTH

PREDICTING WEATHER

Super computers located in Camp Springs, Maryland, are used to predict weather. These computers are fed worldwide weather information, and then make weather forecasts from this data. They create weather maps which are distributed to national weather offices, and to TV and radio stations every 12 hours. Still there is some weather even computers cannot predict.

THE MYSTERY OF TORNADOES

Although weather forecasting is becoming more and more accurate, tornadoes remain a mystery. These storms are more fierce than hurricanes and more destructive than cyclones. At least hurricanes and cyclones can be tracked. People can be warned to get out of the path of these oncoming storms. *Meteorologists*, scientists who study the weather, understand why tornadoes form, but they cannot determine where they will occur.

THE TORNADO APPROACHES

Suppose you spot a thundercloud moving toward you. Swiftly a long, thin piece of cloud, shaped like a funnel, dips down toward you. Suddenly you find yourself looking up into a black hole. Bolts of lightning slice through the empty blackness. The noise you hear is almost impossible to describe. It riddles through the air like hundreds of jets zooming off at one time.

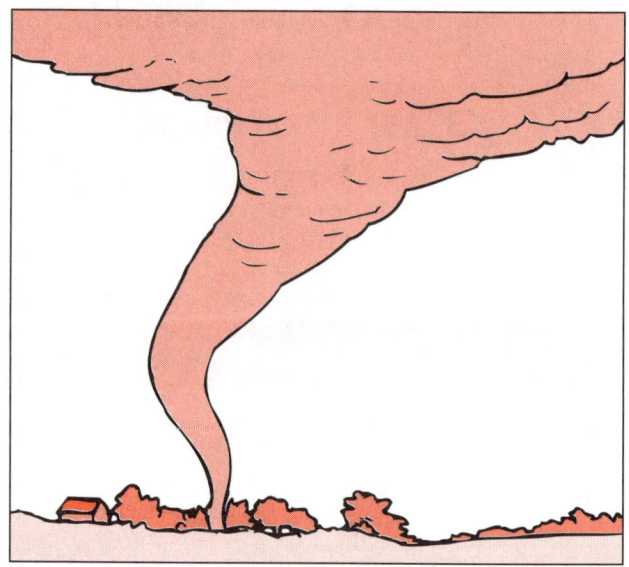

In a magic moment you are saved. The funnel-shaped cloud, or vortex, of the thundercloud does not touch the ground. It lifts up and speeds away. The *rotating*, or spinning, winds can go 300 to 400 miles an hour.

THE TORNADO STRIKES

Off in the distance, the tornado hits the ground. The destruction lasts for only a few minutes. Cars are lifted up and hurled far away. Roofs fly off buildings. Trees are uprooted and sometimes flung miles away. Then, in a flash, the tornado rises up and is gone, leaving bright sunshine behind.

HOW A TORNADO FORMS

Tornadoes occur mainly in the Midwest on the flat plains. There are no mountains to block the flowing air. When cold dry air comes down from Canada (the north), and hot moist air comes up from the Gulf of Mexico (the south), they smash into each other. The cold air tries to push down under the warm air. But the opposite happens. The cold air rides on top of the warm air. It doesn't want to be there. The cold air tries to get below the warm air. Meanwhile the warm air tries to escape. So the cold air and the warm air spin until a whirlwind starts. And there is a big fight in the air.

As long as this activity remains above the ground, no harm is done. If it touches down, the worst storm on Earth occurs.

What I Learned

Circle the letter next to the answer you choose for each question.

1. What is this story mainly about?
   - a. the sky
   - b. meteorologists
   - c. mysteries
   - d. tornadoes

2. What does a meteorologist do?
   - a. study rocks
   - b. study weather
   - c. make super computers
   - d. solve mysteries

3. Why is it most important to be able to predict bad weather?
   - a. to keep good records
   - b. to make a weather map
   - c. to warn people of danger
   - d. to plan vacations

4. Meteorologists are puzzled by tornadoes because they do not know _____.
   - a. why they happen
   - b. how they happen
   - c. when they will happen
   - d. what a funnel is

5. Why do tornadoes form in the Midwest?
   - a. It is warm there.
   - b. There are mountains in the way.
   - c. Nothing stops the winds from meeting.
   - d. It is cold there.

6. A tornado is really a battle between _____.
   - a. hot and cold air
   - b. clean and polluted air
   - c. Mexico and Canada
   - d. sun and heat

7. When does the tornado cause damage?
   - a. at night
   - b. when it touches the ground
   - c. in the air
   - d. when it rains

8. How long does a tornado last?
   - a. a day
   - b. a few minutes
   - c. an hour
   - d. a week

Using the Information
Write a short paragraph for each question below.

Be sure to use details from the story in your answer!

1. Why are tornadoes called "the Worst Storms on Earth"?

_____

_____

_____

_____

_____

2. How are tornadoes different from hurricanes and cyclones?

_____

_____

_____

_____

Using the Information

3. In what part of the U.S. would you be most likely to see a tornado? Explain why.

_____

_____

_____

_____

_____

4. Draw a picture of the inside of the funnel.

Writing Science and social studies books are filled with different types of illustrations: pictures, charts, graphs, and diagrams. They are not there to look pretty. They are important because they help to explain difficult ideas. Often illustrations have an explanation below them. This caption helps us understand the illustration.

Below are a series of illustrations showing tornadoes in several stages. Complete the captions below each picture so that the reader will better understand what happens.

Finish the picture for No. 4 as well!

How Tornadoes Form

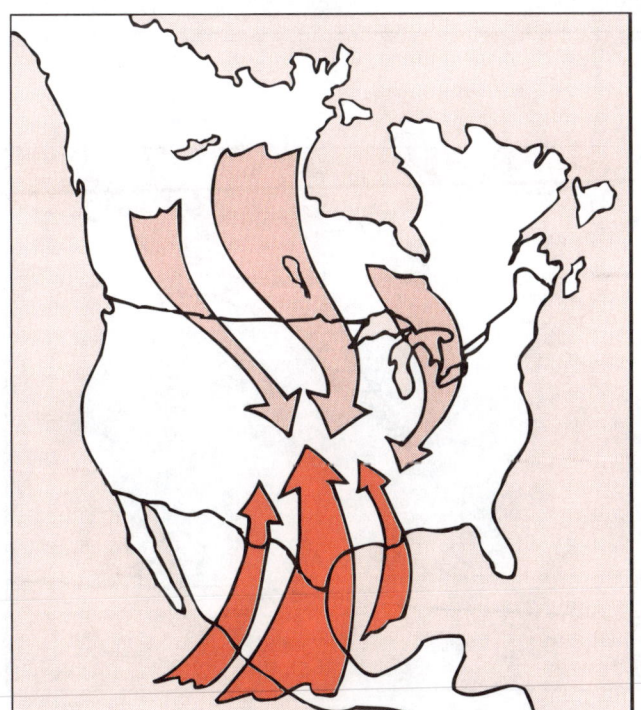

1. A tornado starts when _____ _____ _____

2. In a tornado, the cold air _____ _____ _____

3. When you look up into a tornado, you see _____
_____

You hear _____
_____

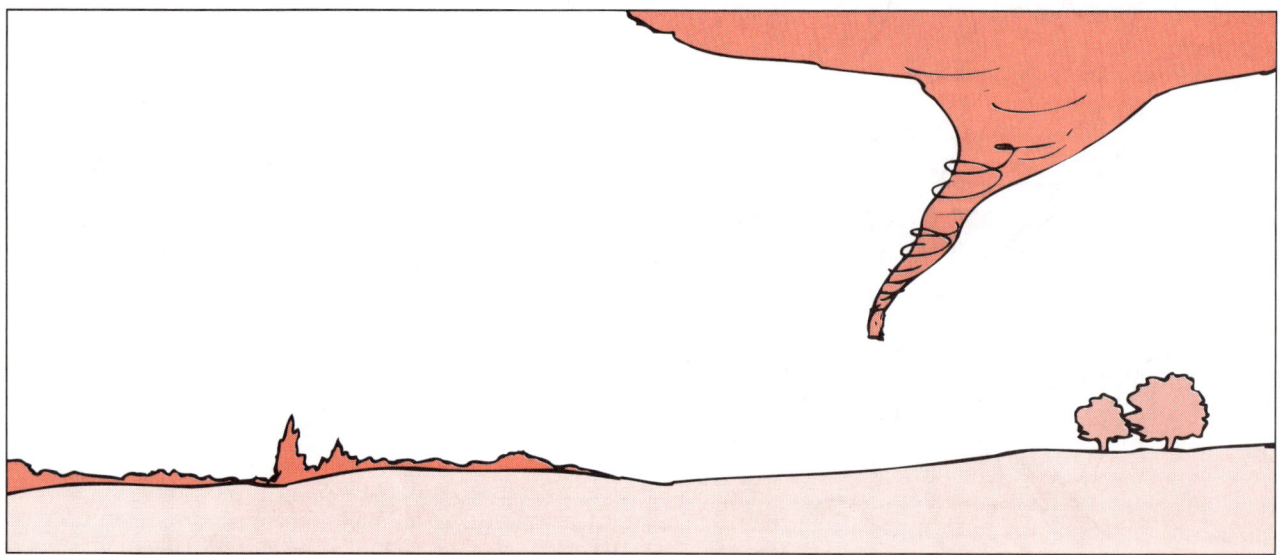

4. After a tornado has left, there is wide damage. _____
_____
_____

Listening Comprehension
HOW THE WORLD GOT WISDOM

Listening Directions

Listen to the African folktale "How the World Got Wisdom." The first time you hear it, listen carefully but do not take notes. The second time you hear the story, write brief notes in the **story map** below. These notes will help you answer some questions about the story.

Title: _____

Setting: _____

Characters: _____

Problem: _____
_____

Events: _____
_____
_____
_____
_____

Solution: _____
_____

Using the Information Write a short paragraph for each question below.

1. Jemani said, "I have collected wisdom from all over the world. Yet a tiny spider is wiser than I am." What did he mean?

_____

_____

_____

_____

2. What was wrong with Jemani's idea about wisdom?

_____

_____

_____

_____

Using the Information

3. Jemani said that wisdom "is still floating through the air. You just have to reach out to grasp it." Explain what he means.

_____

_____

_____

_____

_____

4. In the box below, draw a picture of Jemani's first attempt to climb the tree.

Writing What was Jemani's problem at the beginning of the story? Explain the things he did to try to solve it. Did he succeed?

Remember to look back at your story map for the details!

Go to Editor's Page

A Social Studies Article
THE BOSTON TEA PARTY

What I Know

Fill in the correct circle.

1. A land that is ruled by a country some distance away is called a _____ .
   - ○ state
   - ○ colony

2. A rebellion is a _____ .
   - ○ fight against the government
   - ○ celebration for a new birth

3. England is a part of the country of _____ .
   - ○ Great Britain
   - ○ Scotland

Check the Answer Box to see!

What I Want to Know

(✔ Check all that you want to know.)

- ❏ Why we needed Great Britain
- ❏ Why we rebelled
- ❏ What the Tea Party was all about
- ❏ Who organized this party
- ❏ _____ →

(go on)

ANSWER BOX

1. A land that is ruled by a country some distance away is called a colony.
2. A rebellion is a fight against the government.
3. England is a part of the country of Great Britain.

73

THE BOSTON TEA PARTY

THE REASON FOR COLONIES

Back in the 1700's, Great Britain had colonies in America. These colonies were very important because they helped to support the mother country, England.

The colonies were valuable for two important reasons. They provided cheap raw materials, such as lumber and cotton, for England. The colonies also were a wonderful market for all the things the English produced and needed to sell. The colonists could not manufacture goods like fine furniture, pots and pans, or quality clothing in their new land. They needed to purchase them from England. One of the things they wanted most was tea, the favorite drink in America at that time.

THE TEA TAX

In order to raise even more money from the colonies, King George III of England decided to tax the things the colonists bought. One of these items was tea. The colonists protested. They said that since they couldn't vote in Parliament, the governing body of Great Britain, they did not want to be taxed by the English.

They began to **rebel**[1]. The rebellion started out in a small way. First they bought less tea. But the English would not reduce the tax. Next, the patriots, people who wanted freedom from England,

[1]**rebel**: to fight or struggle against authority or control

refused to allow the ships to unload tea in the harbors of New York and Philadelphia. The governor in Boston, with many English soldiers to assist him, said that the tea could be unloaded in Boston Harbor. He didn't care what the colonists wanted.

THE TEA PARTY PLAN

That did it! On December 16, 1773, Samuel Adams, a great Boston patriot, spoke to over a thousand people at the Old South Meetinghouse, a church in Boston. The people were ready to be convinced. They would support any effort to stop the governor. By that afternoon, Samuel Adams and the patriots, who called themselves the "Mohawks," had **wrapped up**[2] their plans.

THE TEA PARTY

As soon as it was dark, crowds of people met at the docks. The Mohawks had disguised themselves as Indians. They rubbed ashes and black soot on their faces. They wore headbands with feathers. And they let out loud wild war whoops.

People in the crowd held up torches, while the Mohawks boarded three tea ships, tossing two thousand chests of tea into Boston Harbor. Each chest held 320 pounds of expensive tea. Everything else aboard the ships was left unharmed.

King George III of England responded by adding more and higher taxes on imported goods to get revenge for the Boston Tea Party. But that did not stop the colonists. The Boston Tea Party had become a **symbol**[3]. It started Americans on the road to revolution and freedom.

[2]**wrapped up**: finished
[3]**symbol**: a sign; something that stands for an idea

What I Learned

Circle the letter next to the answer you choose for each question.

1. What did England need from the colonies?
   a. raw materials
   b. vacation spots
   c. manufactured goods
   d. tea

2. Why did the colonies need England?
   a. to send tea to
   b. to buy tea from
   c. to give them money
   d. to visit

3. Why do you think the colonists were angry?
   a. They didn't like tea.
   b. They were not getting a fair deal.
   c. The Mohawks liked to fight.
   d. England was so far away.

4. Who were the patriots?
   a. the governors
   b. people who met in churches
   c. people who drank tea
   d. people who wanted the colonies to be free

5. Why was the tea to be unloaded in Boston and not in other cities?
   a. The people in Boston wanted the tea.
   b. Other cities were far away.
   c. The governor didn't listen to the people.
   d. England liked Boston best.

6. What was the Boston Tea Party?
   a. an evening dance
   b. an Indian raid
   c. the start of a rebellion
   d. a party at Samuel Adams' house

7. Who were the Mohawks in this story?
   a. Indians in Boston
   b. rebels in disguise
   c. tea lovers
   d. owners of tea chests

8. Why do you suppose the men dressed up as Indians?
   a. They were at a costume party.
   b. They were actors in a play.
   c. They liked the Indians.
   d. They did not want to be recognized.

Using the Information
Write a short paragraph for each question below.

Be sure to use details from the story in your answer!

1. Why were the colonists so angry?

_____

_____

_____

_____

_____

2. What role did Samuel Adams play in the Boston Tea Party?

_____

_____

_____

_____

_____

Using the Information

3. If you were King George, what would you have done about Boston and the taxes?

_____

_____

_____

_____

_____

4. Draw a picture of at least three things the colonists needed to buy from England.

Pre-Writing

Q.A.D. is a notetaking form that almost looks like a picture. Putting your notes in this format is easy to do and is a good pre-writing technique. Fill in the missing items in the Q.A.D. notes below on the Boston Tea Party.

Question	Answer	Details
1. Why were the colonies valuable to England?	- gave England cheap raw materials - colonists bought England's products	- example: lumber - example: _____
2. What was "Tea Tax"?	- _____	- because England wanted more money - Col. said Eng. had no right to tax them
3. How did they rebel at first?	- bought less tea - then refused to let ships unload	- but Eng. did not lower tax - but _____
4. What did Adams and patriots do about it?	- _____	- _____
5. What happened at Boston Tea Party?	- patriots dumped tea overboard	- dressed as _____ - _____
6. Why was Boston Tea Party important?	- was a symbol	- _____

79

Writing Sometimes you are asked to write a paragraph to answer a question. This is easy to do with your Q.A.D. notes for reminders. The Question and Answer parts make a great beginning. Then fill in the Details. Study the model below.

Question: Why were the colonies valuable to England?

Answer: The American colonies were valuable to England for two important reasons. They gave England the raw materials they needed at a cheap price. Examples of these were lumber and cotton. The colonists also bought many of the products England made. Among them were fine furniture, pots and pans, and nice clothing. These were things the colonists could not make on their own.

Now try one on your own. Use only your Q.A.D. notes.
<u>Do not look back to copy the words of the story.</u>

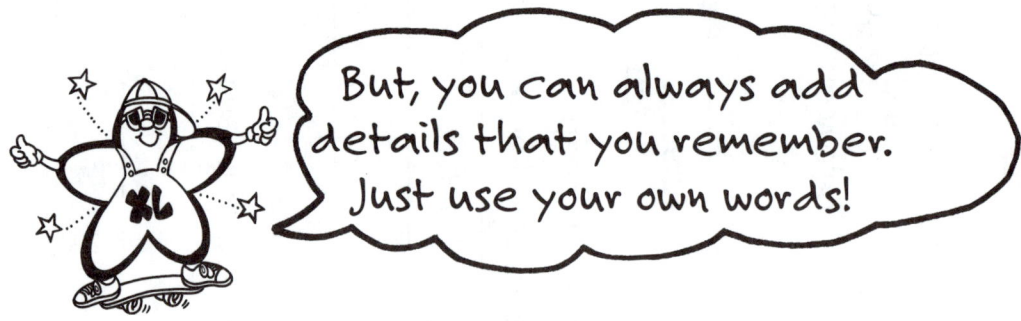

Question: What happened at the Boston Tea Party?

Answer: _____

_____

_____

_____

80

Study Skills

READING A PUBLIC TRANSPORTATION MAP

A public transportation map helps us to find our way by bus, train, boat, or other public transportation. Here is a map of MARTA, the train for the city of Atlanta, Georgia. MARTA helps you to get around the city.

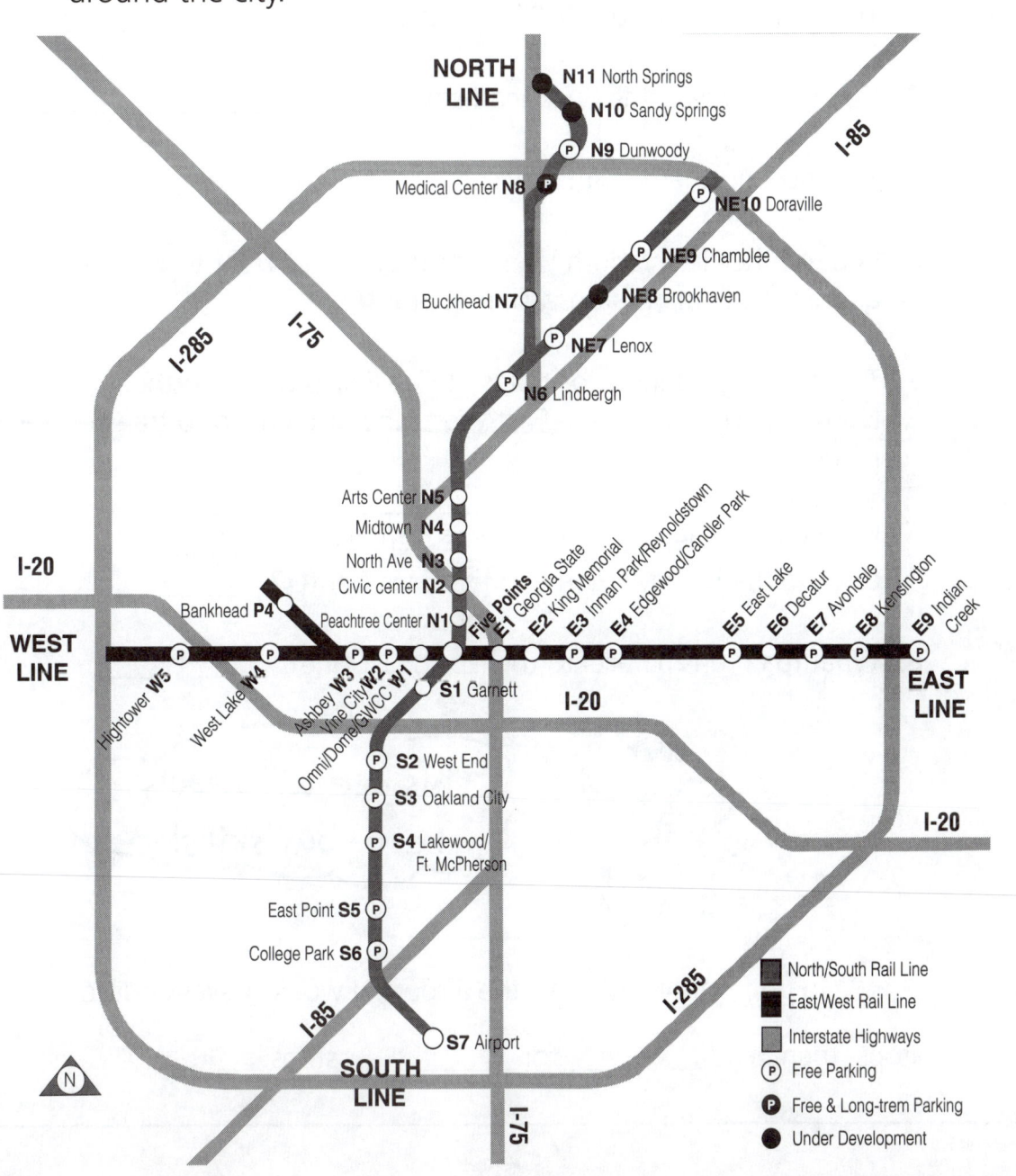

81

What I Learned

Use the map of MARTA to answer the following questions.

1. An interstate highway surrounds most of Atlanta. What is its name? ____

2. Name four train stops that are OUTSIDE that interstate highway.
   _____   _____
   _____   _____

3. The four main lines of MARTA meet at _____.

4. Can I park free at the Buckhead station? _____

5. The most northern point serviced by MARTA is _____.

6. I got on the North/South Line at Midtown and want to go to the airport. How many stops will that be? _____

7. There is a free transfer of trains at Five Points between the North/South Line and the East/West Line. Do I need to transfer trains if I go:
   a. from Decatur to Midtown? _____
   b. from College Park to Peachtree Center? _____
   c. from the King Memorial to the Civic Center? _____

8. What road runs parallel to the Northeast Line? _____

This one will really test your skills!

****To go from Avondale to the airport, I would travel west for _____ stops, then head _____ for _____ stops.

82

Make Your Own Map

Finding your way around a strange town or city can be very difficult. But finding your way around a new school can be tough as well. Make a map of a part of your school so that a new student can navigate, or travel around, the building with ease.

Don't forget to include your classroom.

Questions Use your map to make six good questions that your map will answer.

I started the first one for you!

1. How many doorways do you pass to get from your classroom to the main office? _____

2. _____

3. _____

4. _____

5. _____

6. _____

Can you think of a bonus question? Remember: the answer has to be found on your map!

Bonus: _____

A Poem
THE BAT

What I Know

Fill in the correct circle.

1. A bat sleeps _____ .
   - ○ on its back
   - ○ upside down

2. The poem talks about an "aging" house. This means that the house _____ .
   - ○ is getting old
   - ○ needs work

3. This poem has five "stanzas." This means that it has five ____ .
   - ○ chapters
   - ○ verses

Check the Answer Box to see!

What I Want to Know

(✔ Check all that you want to know.)

- ❏ What animal family the bat is in
- ❏ Where he sleeps
- ❏ When he looks like he's dead
- ❏ When we are most afraid of him
- ❏ _____→

(go on)

ANSWER BOX
1. A bat sleeps upside down.
2. When something is aging, it is getting old.
3. A poem has sections called stanzas or verses.

THE BAT

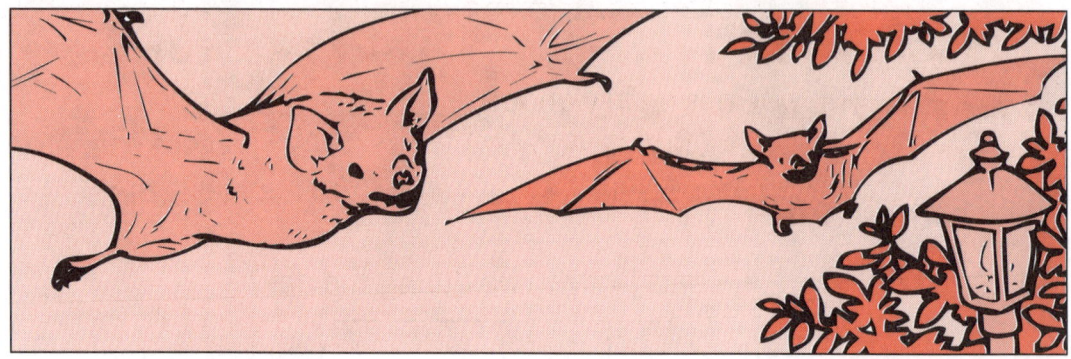

Here is a poem about a bat. Read it carefully **at least two times** before answering the questions.

By day, the bat is cousin to the mouse;

He likes the attic of an aging house.

His fingers make a hat about his head.

His pulse-beat is so slow we think him dead.

He loops in crazy figures half the night

Among the trees that face the corner light.

But when he brushes up against a screen,

We are afraid of what our eyes have seen:

For something is amiss or out of place

When mice with wings can wear a human face.

       by Theodore Roethke

What I Learned

Circle the letter next to the answer you choose for each question.

1. This poem is mainly about _____ .
   - a. a bat and its baby
   - b. scary night animals
   - c. your cousins
   - d. the habits of the bat

2. Where are bats likely to be during the day?
   - a. in an attic
   - b. in a hat
   - c. against a screen
   - d. in the light

3. "He loops in crazy figures half the night" tells us that the bat is ____.
   - a. sitting
   - b. sleeping
   - b. flying
   - d. swimming

4. What happens to the bat when he sleeps?
   - a. He flies in the trees.
   - b. He dies.
   - c. His pulse is slow.
   - d. He brushes up against the screen.

5. The bat travels _____ .
   - a. at noon
   - b. on sunny days
   - c. with the mice
   - d. at night

6. In line 9 the word "amiss" means _____ .
   - a. past
   - b. good
   - c. out of place
   - d. in the attic

7. We are afraid of the bat when we _____ .
   - a. eat him
   - b. hear him
   - c. smell him
   - d. see him

8. You can tell that the poet thinks the bat is _____ .
   - a. friendly
   - b. lovable
   - c. odd
   - d. bashful

Using the Information Write a short paragraph for each question below.

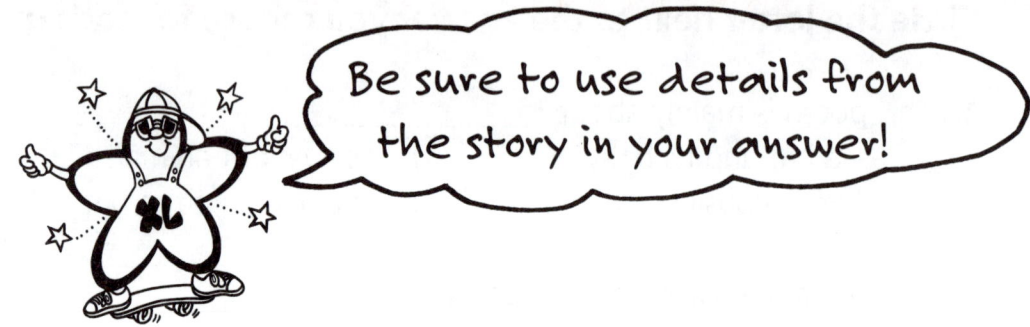

Be sure to use details from the story in your answer!

1. Describe how the bat behaves during the day.

_____
_____
_____
_____
_____

2. Describe the bat's actions at night.

_____
_____
_____
_____

Using the Information

3. What three things in the last line of the poem make the bat seem so scary?

_____

_____

_____

_____

4. When does the poet say we are most scared of the bat? Draw a picture.

89

Pre-Writing The poem tells us that we are often afraid of the bat. Have you ever felt afraid of something that you saw or heard?

Look at the first Mind Map. It shows why we were afraid of the bat. Now complete the second mind map. Show why you were afraid of the thing you saw or heard. Or you can imagine something scary.

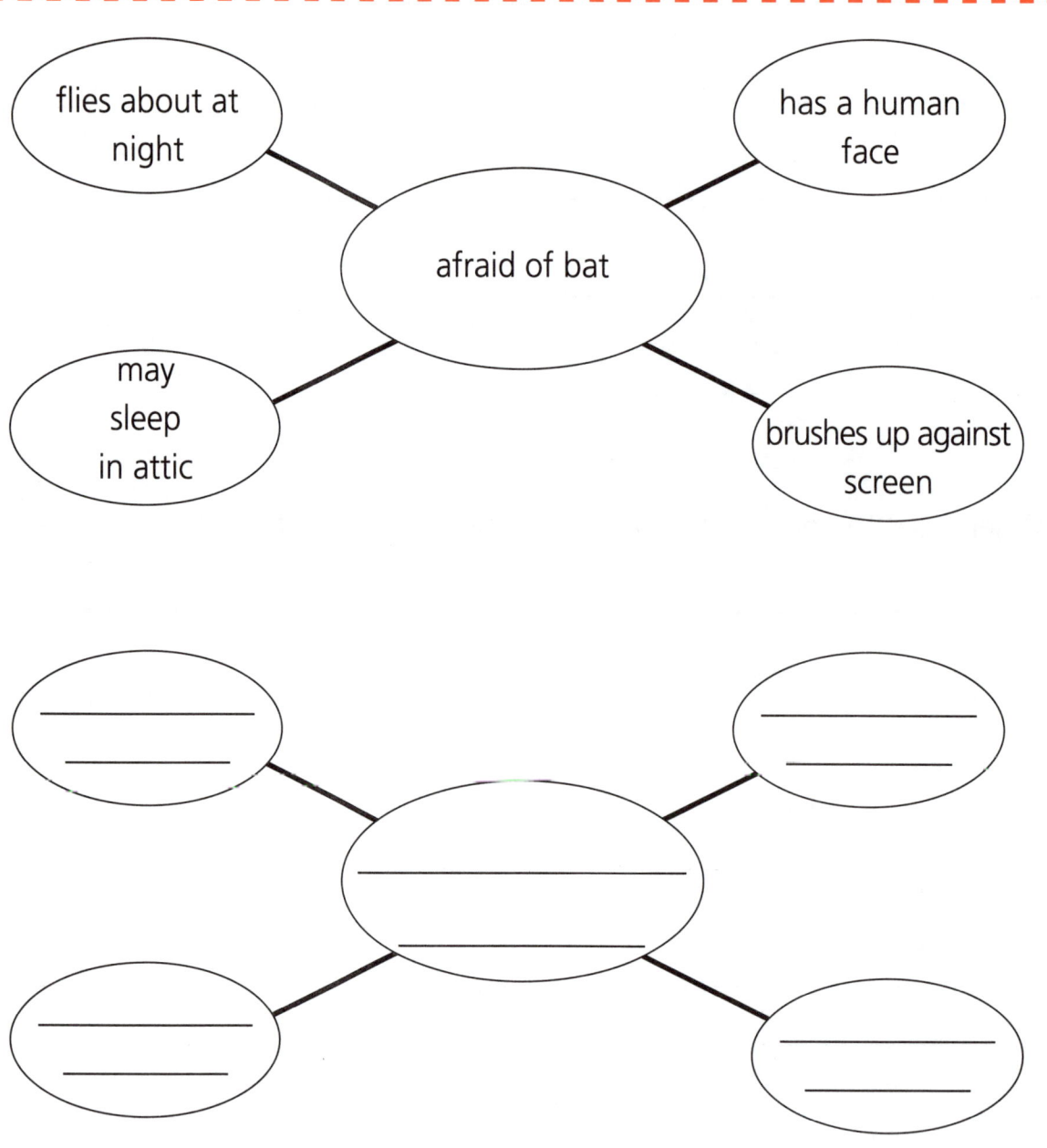

90

Writing Write about the thing that made you afraid. Use your Mind Map to help you. Be sure to tell:
- where it happened.
- when you saw or heard it.
- what it looked like.
- what it did that scared you.

Go to page 92

Go to Editor's Page

Draw the thing that frightened you. Be sure to put in lots of details.

A Biography
BENJAMIN FRANKLIN, PRINTER AND MORE

What I Know

Fill in the correct circle.

1. Benjamin Franklin lived _____ .
   ○ about 50 years ago   ○ about 200 years ago

2. A statesman is someone who has wisdom and skill in _____ .
   ○ medicine   ○ government

3. "Early to bed and early to rise, makes a man healthy, wealthy, and wise" is a famous _____ .
   ○ poem   ○ proverb

Check the Answer Box to see!

What I Want to Know

(✔ Check all that you want to know.)

❑ What Ben Franklin printed
❑ The things Ben is famous for
❑ What Ben did in the government
❑ Who wrote the proverb above
❑ _____

(go on)

ANSWER BOX
1. Benjamin Franklin lived about 200 years ago.
2. A statesman is someone who has wisdom and skill in government.
3. This saying is a famous proverb.

BENJAMIN FRANKLIN, PRINTER AND MORE

EARLY DAYS

Benjamin Franklin was eight years old when he started grammar school in 1714. He was at the top of the class in reading and writing but did poorly in arithmetic. When he was ten, his father said, "It looks like you will not be a good student. I think you should try a trade." So Ben actually went to school for only two years.

THE APPRENTICE

Because Ben loved books, his father thought he should become a printer. When he was ten years old, he became an *apprentice* to his older brother, James, who was in the printing trade. Being an apprentice meant that Ben promised to work for James in his printing shop for a period of nine years.

Ben's job was to clean the shop and the machines. Most importantly, Ben would learn to set type and become a printer. In return, James would give him a place to live, food, and clothes, but no pay. James was a good printer, but he had a nasty temper. He would beat Ben if he did something wrong. But Ben enjoyed the work. Sometimes he and James worked for twelve to fourteen hours to meet deadlines for James' newspaper, *The Courant*.

The Courant was filled with new ideas about life and politics in the new world. It was entertaining, too. By the time Ben was 17, he was *itching* to write articles. He wanted this more than anything else. He knew he would be a good writer. But he also knew James wouldn't print his articles.

BEN, THE AUTHOR

Then he got a brilliant idea, a *brainstorm*! Ben wrote articles using another name, the pen name, Mrs. Silence Dogood. Early in the morning, he slid the sheets of paper under the print shop door. The Mrs. Dogood articles were amusing. They made fun of the showoffs in town and of funny dress styles, like the hoop petticoats women wore under their skirts and the fashionable wigs worn by the men in those days. But they also stuck up for freedom of speech and education for girls.

For a long time no one knew who Silence Dogood was, but the people loved her articles. At last James found out that she really was Ben. He became very, very angry and beat Ben again.

BEN GOES ON HIS OWN

This was the last straw. Ben made his big decision. He stole away, boarded a ship, and ended up in Philadelphia.

The Philadelphians loved him. He was hard working and he was funny. It was not very long before he had a shop where he printed a newspaper of his own, the *Pennsylvania Gazette*. It didn't look like our newspapers. It was a single sheet, folded in half, with news, advertisements, poems, jokes, and advice columns.

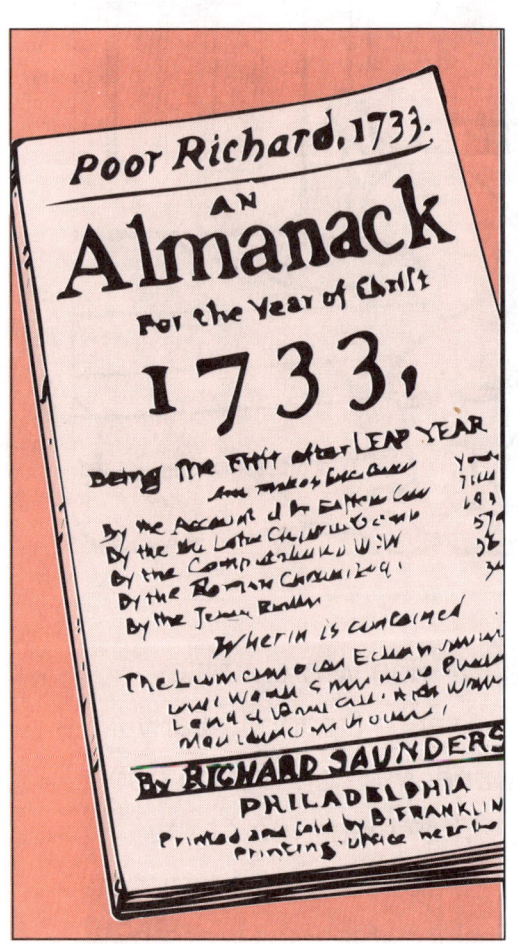

POOR RICHARD IS BORN

Almost every family in the colonies bought an *almanac*, a special kind of calendar that contained recipes, jokes, and little bits of history. People especially liked the astrology, predictions of the future, that were made by studying the stars. Every printer sold them. They knew they would make money on these calendars. Of course, Ben decided to print his own almanac.

Ben called it *Poor Richard's Almanack*, and he printed it every year from 1732 to 1757. It was a best seller in the colonies, all the way from Rhode Island to North Carolina. It made Ben famous for his common sense and *wit*, his ability to say things in an amusing way.

Ben invented Richard Saunders (just as he had invented Silence Dogood). He pretended that Richard wrote the almanac. Richard said he had decided to write an almanac because his wife was always scolding him for looking at the stars, predicting the weather, and not making a living. So he would put his notes and wise sayings into the calendar.

Then he could sell it and make money. "Early to bed and early to rise, makes a man healthy, wealthy, and wise," he advised. "Look ahead or you will look behind," he warned. Other famous sayings were: "God helps them who help themselves." "A word to the wise is enough." "When you are good to others, you are best to yourself." And, "Nothing but money is sweeter than honey."

Poor Richard's Almanack made Ben Franklin rich and famous. Eventually, Ben retired from his job as a printer. But his almanac is still printed today, under the name *Old Farmer's Almanac*.

INVENTOR

Ben could well have spent the rest of his life relaxing and enjoying the money he had earned. But he did not. He was also an inventor. He invented the lightning rod, an instrument that saved houses from being burnt down in a storm. He also invented the Franklin stove, which for the first time could heat a whole house instead of just one room. Today his concept of the bifocal eyeglasses help people see far out on the top and read close up through the bottom.

STATESMAN

Ben Franklin was also involved in our country's fight for freedom. He helped Thomas Jefferson write the Declaration of Independence and signed it in 1776. He went to France to ask for their help to fight the Revolutionary War. The French responded by sending supplies and money. When he died in 1790, Benjamin Franklin was known around the world.

What I Learned

Circle the letter next to the answer you choose for each question.

1. What part of life is this biography mainly about?
    - a. Ben, the Printer
    - b. Ben, the Inventor
    - c. Ben, the Statesman
    - d. Ben, the Runaway

2. Why did Ben become an apprentice?
    - a. He didn't like school.
    - b. He wanted to learn a job.
    - c. He was good at math.
    - d. He wanted to be with his brother.

3. If you said "Ben was itching to write down his brainstorm" you would mean _____ .
    - a. he had a rash on his head
    - b. he wanted to write down a new idea
    - c. he wrote about a storm
    - d. he wanted to get away

4. What did Ben do to get his articles published in *The Courant*?
    - a. He asked his brother.
    - b. He made his own newspaper.
    - c. He made up a pen name.
    - d. He delivered them by mail.

5. What happened because of the "Silence Dogood" articles?
    - a. Ben ran away.
    - b. James gave him a better job.
    - c. People didn't buy the paper.
    - d. Ben bought some straw.

6. Newspaper printers wrote only news. How did Ben get to write his famous sayings?
    - a. He sent letters.
    - b. He made up "Poor Richard."
    - c. He went to North Carolina
    - d. He went to bed early.

7. Ben was famous for his wit. That means he was _____.
    - a. old
    - b. strong
    - c. ferocious
    - d. funny

8. Which of the following did Ben NOT invent?
    - a. the lightning rod
    - b. the Franklin stove
    - c. bifocal glasses
    - d. the telephone

Using the Information

Write a short paragraph for each question below.

Be sure to use details from the story in your answer!

1. What was *Poor Richard's Almanack* all about?

_____

_____

_____

_____

2. Why is Ben Franklin considered such a great statesman?

_____

_____

_____

_____

Using the Information

3. Ben was a printer, inventor, and statesman. Which do you think was his most important job? Why?

_____

_____

_____

_____

_____

4. Draw a picture of the real Richard Saunders and Silence Dogood articles.

They are really _____.

100

Pre-Writing Poor Richard wrote many proverbs in his almanac. Choose the one you think is best and explain it below.

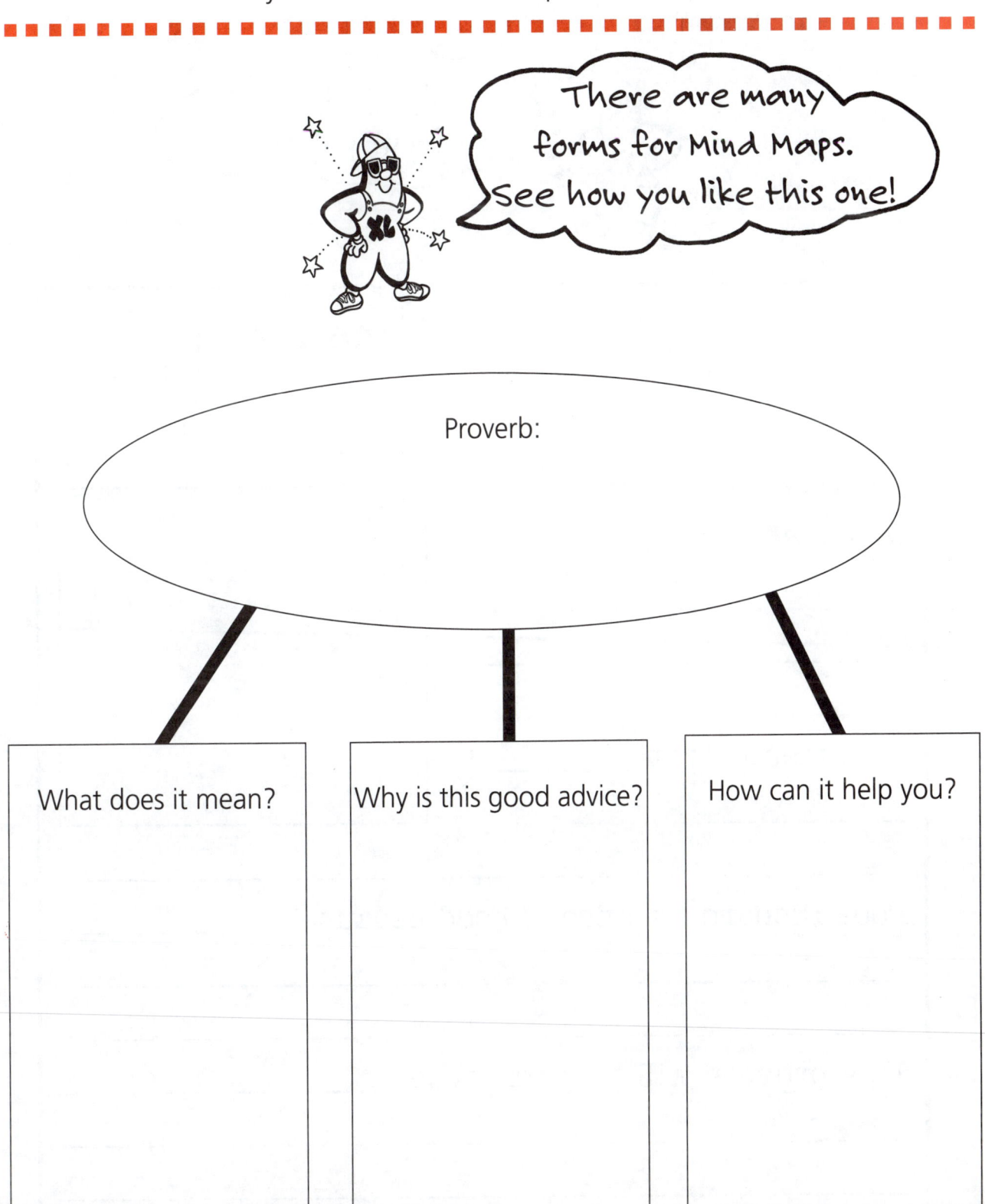

Writing Use your Mind Map notes to help you write an article for your own almanac.

_____'s Almanac
(your pen name)

Latest News – Advice – Predictions   Price:

My good friend, Poor Richard, once said,
"_____
_____
_____

This means that _____
_____

Poor Richard's advice is good because _____
_____
_____

This proverb will help you when _____
_____
_____

102   Go to Editor's Page

A Study Skill
READING A TIME LINE

A time line shows events in the order in which they happened. It helps us to view things in their correct sequence.

The time line below shows some interesting dates from our nation's history. Study it carefully. Then use it to answer the questions on the next page.

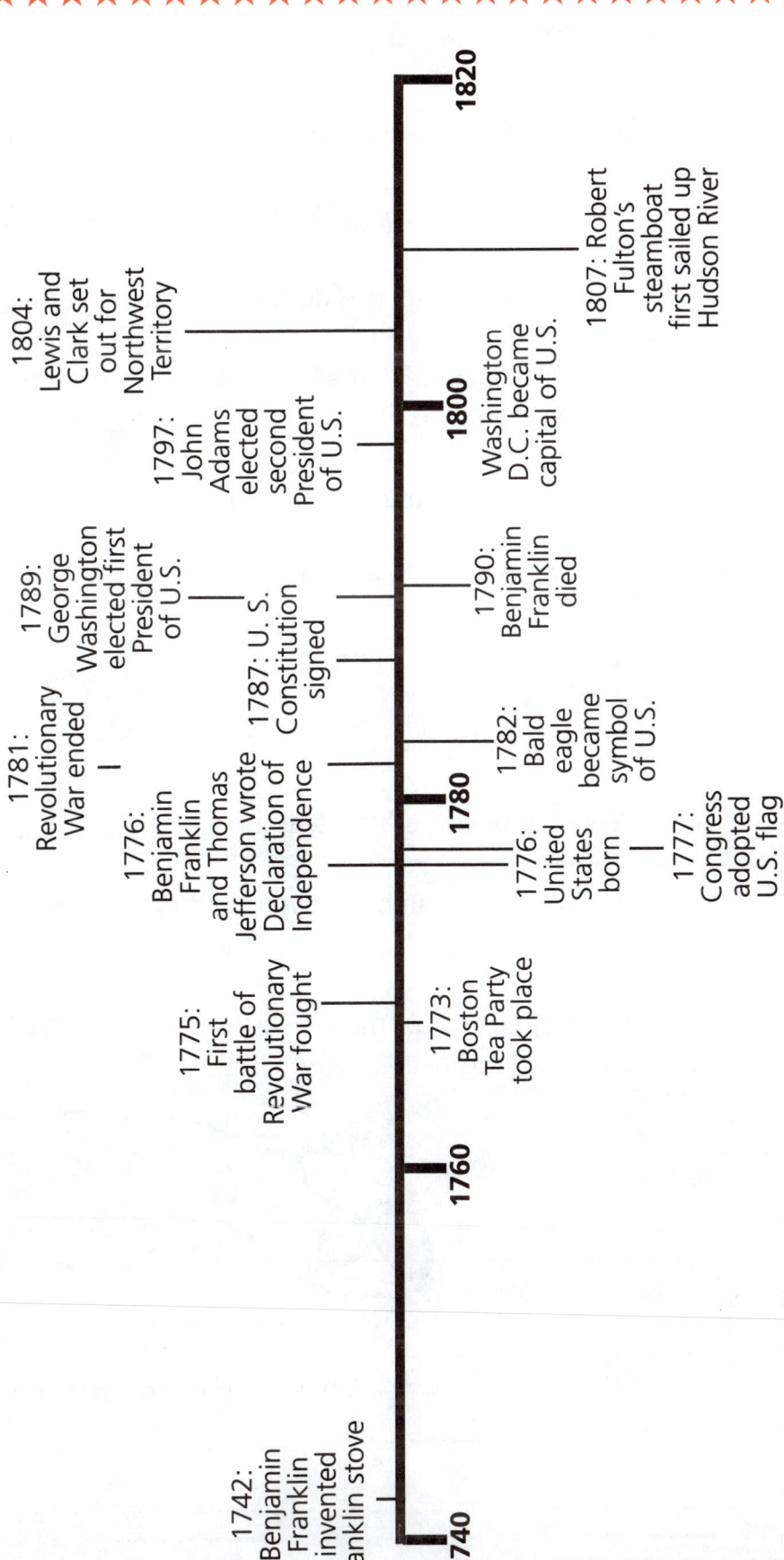

What I Learned

Use the time line to find the answer to each question below.

1. When was George Washington elected President? _____

2. How long was President Washington's term of office? _____

3. Who helped Thomas Jefferson write the Declaration of Independence? _____

4. How long did the Revolutionary War last? _____

5. Which bird is the symbol of our country? _____

6. Where is the capital of our country? _____

7. When was the site for our capital chosen? _____

8. Who built the first steamboat? _____

9. Was the steamboat invented during Benjamin Franklin's lifetime? _____

10. A span of how many years is shown on this time line? _____

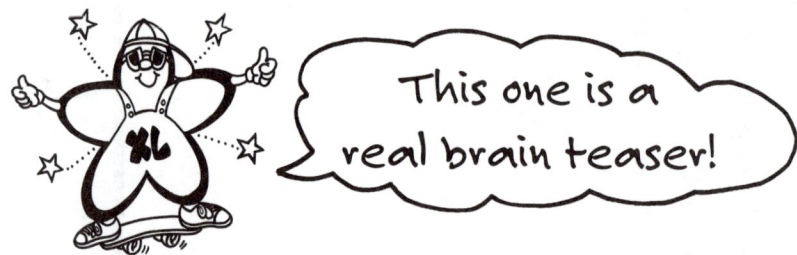

**** How many years before your birth was our country born? _____

104

Make Your Own Time Line

Time lines can be fun!

Make a time line of all the special events that happened in your life.

Start the time line with your birth.

Try to think of six things you will want to remember when you are old, such as . . . .

○ when you got your first two-wheel bike
○ when you moved (or your best friend moved)
○ the best party ever
○ the year your team did great

Make sure you put in all the regular dates, too!

Questions

Make up at least five good questions based on your time line.
Make sure that the questions can be answered by the time line alone!

1. How old was I when _____

2. _____

3. _____

4. _____

5. _____

How about a good bonus question? Make them think!

**** BONUS _____

106

EDITOR'S PAGE

Congratulations! You have written a wonderful **first draft**. But it really is just a *first* draft of a soon to be wonderful essay. Follow the checklists that follow to add some sparkle.

Read your completed essay *aloud*.

Y   N   **Did you stick to the topic?**
(Does every sentence belong?)
(Cut out any stray sentences!)

Y   N   **Can you think of a better way to say some things?**
(Just cross them out. Change and add details!)

Y   N   **Is the first sentence a good one?**
(Arrows will change this easily!)

Y   N   **Can you add descriptive adjectives and adverbs?**
(Underline a few plain nouns and verbs. Then go back and think of some exciting describing words for them. Use the ^ sign to show where they go!)

Y   N   **Did you use the same word over and over again?**
(Do 3 sentences in a row start the same?)
(If you can't think of changes, try a thesaurus!)

Remember, your first try is never your best. Bet it sounds much better now!

107

Check your writing for errors.

Y   N   **Do you use complete and clear sentences?**
                      (If unsure, ask a friend!)

Y   N   **Is the punctuation of each sentence correct?**
                      (Check for **. ? !**)

Y   N   **Did you use quotes (" ") when your characters talk?**

Y   N   **Are there capitals where needed?**
                      (Check: beginning of sentence, proper nouns, initials.)

Y   N   **Is the spelling of all words correct?**
                      (If unsure, check the dictionary!)

Your essay is now complete. If you want to share your work with others, it should be written orderly and clearly. Copy your essay onto a clean sheet of paper.

Be sure to include all the changes and corrections you've made.